P9-BZR-609

The Eternal Choice We All Must Make

PAT BOONE

Defender
Crane, MO

IF anyone serves Me, let him follow me;
And where I am, there my servant
will be also.

IF anyone serves Me,
Him my Father will honor.

~John 12:26

And **IF** anyone hears My words and
does not believe, I do not judge him;

For I did not come to judge the world,
But to save the world.

He who rejects Me, and does not
receive my words,

Has that which judges him—
the word that I have spoken

Will judge him in the last day.

-John 12:47, 8

Behold, I am coming quickly!

Blessed is he who keeps the prophecy of this book.

He who is unjust, let him be unjust still; he who is filthy let him be filthy still; he who is righteous, let him be righteous still; he who is holy, let him be holy still.

For I testify to everyone who hears the words of the prophecy of this book:

IF anyone adds to these things, God will add to him the plagues that are written in this book,

And **IF** anyone takes away from the words of the book of this prophecy,

God will take away his part from the book of life,
From the holy city—

And from the things which are written in this book:
I am coming quickly

He who testifies to these things says, "Surely I am coming quickly."

~Jesus, in Revelation 22

IF: The Eternal Choice We All Must Make
by Pat Boone

Defender Publishing Crane, MO 65633 ©20209

ISBN: 9781948014458

A CIP catalog record of this book is available from the Library of Congress.

Cover design by Jeffrey Mardis.

Unless otherwise noted, all Scripture quoted is from New King James Version

Contents

Foreword

You know the story; you've probably heard it a million times—especially when you were a kid. It's the one about Noah and the ark.

The story, found in Genesis 6 and 7, is historically factual. The human race God created had spread out over the then-known world, but was increasingly unresponsive to their Creator. In fact, as the account goes, not only were people indifferent to God, but they were becoming selfish, violent, and corrupt. God began to see that "every thought in their hearts was evil continually. He was grieved in His heart"—and that was long before the time when social media, easily accessible pornography, and violent video games made "evil" thoughts and deeds even more convenient, as they are today.

So, in the middle of that story, we come to this alarmingly strong statement: "And the Lord was sorry that He had made man on the earth" (Genesis 6:6).

The people were a terrible disappointment to God! He actually said, “My Spirit shall not strive with man forever” (Genesis 6:3).

So He decided to start all over.

Friend, let this sink in, will you? *God decided to start all over.*

I hope you know the rest of the story: God made a way to save the only faithful and obedient man he could find from the coming destruction by giving him the remarkable task of building a gigantic boat. The project took five-hundred-year-old Noah about a hundred years to complete. Then he herded his family of eight and a lot of animals and birds aboard, shut the vessel’s massive doors and windows…

…and the rains came.

Noah and his family were preserved through the Flood that wiped out all life from the inhabited earth. That is, it wiped out *all life but the eight members of Noah’s family*!

Just eight human beings survived God’s judgment.

Does this story get your attention, as it does mine? This is God Himself we’re talking about here, and He doesn’t mess around. When He says, “The game is over,” it’s over. And when He makes a list of those who are acceptable to Him, *it can be a very short list.*

God has been making a new list for a long, long time now, and my name is on it.

I want to make sure yours is on it, too.

That's why I had to write this book.

And perhaps that's why you're reading it.

◊◊◊

For some time now, I've felt compelled to write this book—but I didn't really want to. I struggled against it and put it off, hoping that someone else would do it. But as far as I'm aware, hardly anybody but a few very bold preachers want to do it, either. It's become an uncomfortable, highly unpopular sermon topic, except actually in church, among those who already believe.

It certainly is the most important thing any of us can—and must—consider, but you can clear any room if you bring it up!

That is, few folks want to be blunt and direct about *where we go when we die* and about how we can make the biggest decision we'll ever make in our lives. It's an eternally fixed decision, *and you're making it right now*—maybe unknowingly.

But this idea has been burning a hole in me, and I now believe God wants it done. He's looking at me, urging me to write what has to be written and to say what needs to be said—because HE's already said it—and very few seem to want to hear it. It's all there in the Holy Bible. It's been there for centuries.

But who reads that "outdated" book now?

Do you?

Do you by chance have one of the millions of Bibles that have the actual words Jesus spoke printed in red letters? Those red letters remind us that the disarmingly blunt, often shocking things Jesus said were actual quotes, not a biblical scholar's "idea" of what He said.

If you have read those words in red, have you paid any special attention to them? Has it sunk in that the very Son of God, the Word made flesh in human form—*God Himself*—is using them to speak to *you*?

Are you of a religious persuasion other than Christianity and feel that nothing Jesus said matters to you, anyway? Have you become disenchanted with "religion" in any and all of its forms? Are you, like millions of others today, really just "too busy" to think seriously about God—if He really does exist—and about what He might expect of you if He does?

Do you see yourself as a "good person" who is nice to others (at least to the ones you like), and who usually tries to do the "right thing"?

Isn't that enough? Is it enough to make sure your name is written on the short list of people who will be saved from the coming destruction—who will be saved for all of eternity?

The clock is ticking, and recent crises and world calamities are just a prelude to what's coming.

if

If you have, at any time, thought seriously about religion, have you wondered whether one faith system is any better than another? Some folks say, "Hey, all religions lead to the same place; they all worship the same God."

Does that sound good to you?

Are you among the millions today who resent people who claim that "their way" is "the only way," and who say that following some other belief will land you in hell after you die? Maybe you'd rather just skip the whole conversation until you're older. Maybe then, you'll feel the need to choose one belief system or another. And if you don't, then, *so what*?

Do you privately believe in a "Higher Power" or a Creator God, an omnipotent Being who made everything there is and set it all in motion, one who knows about us individually and who cares enough about us to be involved with us in any way—like "the Force" who is "with us" from the *Star Wars* series?

If you're not *sure* there actually is a God, do you secretly hope there is? And do you hope that, somehow, He may like you? Be good to you? Welcome your friendship and fellowship for all eternity?

Let's get down to it: *What do you believe, really?* And what are those beliefs based on? Has someone you admire or respect, a person who seems to "have it all together," convinced you that all religion is just wishing, grasping for someone or something bigger than you who can make up for what you lack? Maybe that person has said you should just buck up, depend on yourself, and maybe, just maybe, you'll come out a winner without leaning on a "made-up," "nonexistent" God.

If any of the above describes you, I'm writing this book for you. I care about you. I can even say—truthfully—that I love you, though we likely haven't met.

I can also honestly say that I've been where you are: I've had the same questions, the same doubts, the same frustrations at being told I have to believe something I can't see, I have to just "take it on faith," and I have to stake my eternal destiny on ideas and teachings that *may not be true*!

How can I—how can *you*—know?

Well, I *do* know. Now. Undeniably and with certainty. That's why I've felt this insistence to share the information in this book with you and any others who will listen.

If you're a rational person, one who can think for yourself without looking at someone else to tell you whether you're right or wrong, if you can just look at the evidence I'm going to share with you and make your decisions on incontrovertible facts, you *will* know three things:

1. **God exists.** Science proves this. He's real, and He is the Designer, the Creator, the Source of everything there is.

2. **The Bible is the Word of God.** It is divinely inspired and authored through inspired men.

3. **Jesus is the Son of God, the promised Messiah of Israel.** He is the Savior of all men and women who dare to believe in Him and follow Him through this short, muddled life.

Have I lost you?

Do you think this is just too huge a topic, beyond the intelligence and depth of one guy like me for you to take seriously (especially because, if I'm right, it may shake up long-held views and cherished concepts that you may have clung to for most of your life)?

Well, I've already done it once. Several years ago, I wrote, with a research writer for *Investors' Business Daily* and other scholarly papers, a book called *Questions about God...and Answers That Could Change Your Life.*

In that paperback, I accomplished my purposes on all three counts, sharing the scientific proof that God exists, the Bible is the Word of God, and Jesus is the Son of God.

In fact, on one occasion after the book was published, my wife and I were observing a lovely Passover Seder in the home of our family doctor. I was surprised to hear the Orthodox Jewish physician say to all of his guests, "Listen, family and friends. I'm holding in my hands a book written by our guest Pat Boone. I've read it carefully once, and now

I'm reading it again. *I want you all to have a copy of it and read it.*"

When the ceremony was over and we were eating, one of the doctor's relatives came to me and asked what the book was about. I answered, "If you have read the fifty-third chapter of Isaiah in your Bible, you'll know exactly what it's about."

The kind man looked puzzled, so I opened my Bible and turned to the beginning of that chapter—actually starting with the last three verses of chapter 52, all of which Jewish scholars know is about a coming Messiah, a Savior—and handed it to him, asking him to read it aloud, which he did:[1]

Who has believed our report?
And to whom has the arm of the LORD been revealed?
For He shall grow up before Him as a tender plant,
And as a root out of dry ground.
He has no form or comeliness;
And when we see Him,
There is no beauty that we should desire Him.
He is despised and rejected by men,
A Man of sorrows and acquainted with grief.
And we hid, as it were, our faces from Him;
He was despised, and we did not esteem Him.
Surely He has borne our griefs
And carried our sorrows;
Yet we esteemed Him stricken,

Smitten by God, and afflicted.
But He was wounded for our transgressions,
He was bruised for our iniquities;
The chastisement for our peace was upon Him,
And by His stripes we are healed.
All we like sheep have gone astray;
We have turned, every one, to his own way;
And the LORD has laid on Him the iniquity of us all.
He was oppressed and He was afflicted,
Yet He opened not His mouth;
He was led as a lamb to the slaughter,
And as a sheep before its shearers is silent,
So He opened not His mouth.
He was taken from prison and from judgment,
And who will declare His generation?
For He was cut off from the land of the living;
For the transgressions of My people He was stricken.
And they made His grave with the wicked—
But with the rich at His death,
Because He had done no violence,
Nor was any deceit in His mouth.
Yet it pleased the LORD to bruise Him;
He has put Him to grief.
When You make His soul an offering for sin,
He shall see His seed, He shall prolong His days,
And the pleasure of the LORD shall prosper in His
hand.
He shall see the labor of His soul, and be satisfied.

By His knowledge My righteous Servant shall justify
many,
For He shall bear their iniquities.
Therefore I will divide Him a portion with the great,
And He shall divide the spoil with the strong,
Because He poured out His soul unto death,
And He was numbered with the transgressors,
And He bore the sin of many,
And made intercession for the transgressors.

When the gentleman had finished reading the words, he said in a hushed voice, "Why—this is about Jesus!"

And it is; *it couldn't be about anyone else.*

I agreed, and suggested that he read my book to understand the context and substance of what he, a practicing Jew, had just read and comprehended for the first time in his life.

That evening, I made up my mind to do this book.

Why? Because it's so obvious that good, well-meaning, busy, twenty-first-century people—by the millions—*just don't know who God really is,* what He expects—nay, demands—from each of us, and how He has provided the Way for us to know beyond doubt that our names are on His relatively short list!

So please—*please*—read on.

Part I

My Personal Journey

chapter one

Who Am I to Write a Book Like This?

First things first: So, who am I to write a book like this?

Good question.

May I introduce myself in my typical, long-winded way? (And if you already know who I am, for better or worse, feel free to just skip over the next several pages of autobiography.)

For the next few minutes, I may sound like just a "lucky" guy who happened to be able to sing, make some big movies, have a successful career, and raise a wonderful family. At the risk of seeming to brag, I've decided to lay it all out, to tell in some detail how very fortunate I've been—in the hope of convincing you that I may have learned things you really need to know.

My life has been miraculous—and I *know* it's not by coincidence. The Creator God has proved Himself real to me—and I want Him to do the same for you.

Actually, I've pretty much abandoned my use of the word "lucky" for a long time now. Instead, I refer to myself as "blessed." In fact, I would say I'm "*greatly* blessed." That change in self-description stems from a sobering experience—and my subsequent search for what I really believe—that took place in the 1960s, when I was in my early thirties and on a world concert tour that took me to Thailand.

Things on the road were going great. Record sales were solid, shows in many countries were selling out, and I was a quintessential happy-go-"lucky" guy.

But one day in Bangkok, Thailand, during a resting day between shows, I came across three Buddhist monks in a public square. To my horror, I saw that *they had doused themselves with kerosene and set themselves on fire.*

They were silently burning themselves alive.

I couldn't look, and I couldn't look away.

"Why are they doing this?" I frantically asked my Thai guide.

"I'm not quite sure," he said, "but they are very dedicated Buddhists who are trying to draw public attention to the poor and the needy as a dramatic, all-out expression of their faith. I think they want to persuade others to believe what they believe."

I was aghast, shaken, and bewildered.

What kind of faith was this?

What drove these men to end their own lives in such a horrific way, when they could never know if their actions had accomplished any good?

My mind went immediately to a verse of Scripture I knew well, from the famous chapter on love in 1 Corinthians 13:3: "And though I bestow all my goods to feed the poor, *and though I give my body to be burned, but have not love, it profits me nothing*" (emphasis added).

The words seared my consciousness...and my conscience.

Personal Crisis of Faith

Did I have as much faith as those monks in what *I* believed? What *did* I believe, anyway? These monks had been taught a belief system and were willing to give their lives for it. Would I be prepared to do the same? Would I be willing to give my life for what I believed?

In far different and much better circumstances, I had also been taught a faith system. I thought mine was better, but how did I know if that was true? Had my parents and some preachers or teachers simply convinced me of what to believe? How could I prove—*for myself alone*—that what I believed was real, that what I believed was true, and that what I believed was strong enough to confidently stake my whole life on, now and into eternity?

Starting Over

So—I decided to start my spiritual journey from scratch. I tried to "erase" everything I'd been taught about faith, and then, on a blank page in my mind, I formulated three basic questions:

- How do I know there's a God?
- What about the Bible itself?
- What about Jesus?

I devoted many hours to extensive research, much prayer, and carefully considered, objective thought—and ultimately resolved my three basic questions about God, the Bible, and Jesus for myself. I prayed for God to somehow save and reward the monks I had seen in Bangkok for their sacrifice, believing they were doing His will, and I renewed my own commitment to Him.

I've now read the Bible cover to cover, every word, almost every year since then (thirty-five years now, and continuing).

And I've resolved to try, in every way I can, to convince everyone I can reach of the truths God has shown me. That's what compels me to write this book.

Believe me, YOU AND YOUR ETERNAL DESTINY are why I'm writing this right now!

So please stay with me; we're just getting started.

chapter two

Blue Moon Boone

Okay, back to the question we first asked in the previous chapter: Who am I to write this book?

Here we go.

Growing up in Nashville, Tennessee, I never dreamed of making movies or becoming an actor. I didn't even know I could act! I just loved to sing, for the fun of it, in family gatherings and in school programs, whenever a guy who could carry a tune was called for.

I remember, though, seeing Bing Crosby in a couple of movies, and I was impressed with how easy he made it seem to start singing in the middle of a comic or romance scene, as if it was the most natural thing. So, I soon became a fan. My parents had some of his records, and I'd play 'em just for the enjoyment, sometimes singing along and crooning the way he did. It seemed to come easy for me, too.

One Saturday afternoon when I was twelve, a friend's mom took us to the Belle Meade Theater in an upscale Nashville neighborhood to see a Western movie. Before the film started, three kids performed a live stage show—singing, tap dancing, and playing an instrument. The theater manager, Ed Jordan, a former vaudevillian performer, emceed, letting the audience of mostly preteens decide the show's winner by measure of their applause, shouts, or raucous jeers. It was a tough crowd of kids who mostly weren't impressed with either contestant; they just wanted to get on to the movie!

But there was a prize for the winner—a banana split at the drugstore next to the theater.

Now *that* got my attention!

I asked how you got to be on the show, and learned that you had to make it to a local dance studio sometime during the week to audition for Elizabeth Bryant Combes, a former professional dancer who ran the studio. One of her students was always one of the three contestants.

So, my friend's mom took me to audition, and my performance of a Bing Crosby song landed me a spot on the program the very next Saturday. When it was my turn to take the stage, I nervously stood offstage, looking and listening as that wild bunch of boys running up and down the aisles, pulling girls' hair, throwing popcorn, and just plain cutting up were waiting to give us competitors a hard time.

But Mr. Jordan quieted the group, telling them that a "new Bing Crosby" (I'm pretty sure they didn't know the "old" Bing, but the name sounded important, I guess) was about to sing for them.

"Sit down and *get quiet*!" he said. To my surprise, they did.

I won the banana split!

With that, I was hooked. For the next couple of years, I kept learning the latest pop hits and singing them for "Miz Combes," who would put me on with a dancer and some other kid—each of us hoping to get that banana split, which I did several more times.

From time to time, one of the mothers at the performances would ask me to come sing for her sewing club, book club, or Shakespeare club, so I would happily accept those gigs, accompanied by a piano teacher, Ruth Mowry. Then I "graduated" to getting invitations to sing for Rotary Club or Junior Chamber of Commerce luncheons, and for some reason I'd do it—again, accompanied by Ruth, who always made time to play for me.

We never asked for pay—and none was ever offered. If we got a nice lunch out of an engagement, we were happy. We performed just for the fun of doing it, and because we could. I could never think of an excuse to say no, even though I stayed busy with sports and studying to make all A's in my classes. Singing pop songs for happy listeners just made me feel good.

In high school, even before I met Shirley during my junior year, I became known as "Blue Moon Boone"—because whenever there was an occasion, I could sing that old Bing Crosby song, "Blue Moon," with no accompaniment, and the kids seemed to like it. I entered a number of talent shows in Nashville, and almost always came in second behind a pianist, a violinist, or a classically trained vocalist who had obviously worked at developing a skill and got more applause.

I just sang pop songs—and *anybody* could do that, right?

But in my senior year, when I was almost eighteen, I won first place in a talent night at East High. The prize was a trip to New York City to audition for the *Ted Mack Amateur Hour*, a national program on Saturday night TV that was a forerunner of shows like *American Idol* and *America's Got Talent*.

Like I said earlier, I had always come in second during other competitions, so I was more surprised than anybody that I won. I even tried to get the judges to send Shirley McGauhey to New York instead of me, because she had been classically trained and had done a great song that night. She was crying about her loss backstage. But the judges said no—they wanted *me* to represent Nashville on national television.

Publicity shot for a 14-year-old local singer

So I did. Winners were determined by the number of cards and letters of support received from viewers, and I won—three weeks in a row!

That's when I started thinking about singing as a career.

But by then, I was in love with a girl named Shirley Foley.

High-School Sweethearts

Shirley had transferred from West High to David Lipscomb, the Christian high school I was attending in Nashville, and we had met as sixteen-year-olds under the old grandfather clock in the school's Harding Hall. So, I found the idea of singing for a living intriguing, but I knew it wasn't the type of a career you could count on—especially since I was already trying to decide how I might support a wife and family.

As Shirley and I talked and dreamed and tried to envision a life together, we decided I'd become a teacher/preacher like my role models at Lipscomb. We made plans to go to college together, graduate at the same time, get married, and settle into a quiet, local life; she would raise our kids and I would help other young people get a good start in life by teaching them to live according to Christian principles.

Sixteen-year-old Pat and Shirley falling in love

Shirley's dad, Red Foley, was a Country Music Hall of Fame singer, so she had seen firsthand the rigors and pressures of entertaining and all that profession demanded. She knew she didn't want that kind of lifestyle for her future. Becoming a teacher's wife sounded great to her.

With the father of the bride, Country Hall of Famer Red Foley

Then Shirley's mother died after suffering through a long, untreatable heart condition. Red took an offer to move his three daughters to Springfield, Missouri, to start the *Ozark Jubilee* national country music show on Saturday nights.

My Shirley was being taken away, and soon, and neither of us could accept it.

So, when we were just nineteen years old, a week before the Foleys moved to Missouri, I asked Shirley to marry me. She said yes, then we asked her dad for his permission, and he bought our rings. That was that: I would teach, and she enrolled in nurses' training.

End of story...

...or so we thought.

Soon after we were married, Shirley and I packed all our possessions (we didn't have much) into a U-Haul trailer and headed to Denton, Texas, so I could enroll in North Texas State University, a noted music school where I would prepare for my life as a high school English teacher and maybe a vocal coach.

We had no sooner unpacked than we found out that Shirley was expecting our first child!

What did Shirley and I know about marriage and creating and raising a family? Precious little, except what we'd seen in our parents, and what we'd learned in attending church and reading God's Word as we grew. We just decided we'd pattern our lives on what I

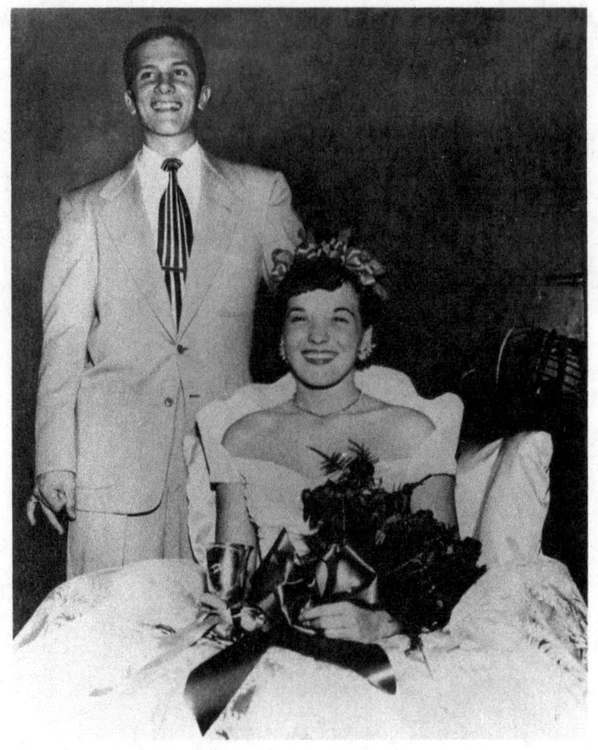

The beginning of a sixty-five-year, happy marriage

called "Tennessee Standards"—be Bible-believing and Bible-living, the best we could.

So far, so good, we felt. Ahead of schedule, our family was beginning to grow, and we were thrilled.

But wait!

if

A Change in Direction

A producer from the *Ted Mack Show* called to let me know I needed to go back to New York to compete with the other three-time winners. This time, the prize was enough cash to pay for my college education. So I scurried back to New York and sang well; I believed I had a good chance of winning—but during the days when we were waiting for the card and letter votes to be counted, I went on—and won—the *Arthur Godfrey Talent Scouts* show!

That sounds like great news, but that performance cost me—big time. The win disqualified me from winning the *Ted Mack Show*—and all I got for winning the *Godfrey* show was four mornings on his morning CBS show and a plane ticket home.

I left New York believing I had totally ruined my big chance at a singing career.

Disheartened, I stopped off in Nashville on my way back to Denton to commiserate with my folks, only to find out that Randy Wood of Dot Records had called to offer me a record contract.

My first record was "Two Hearts, Two Kisses," which became a million-selling, top-ten hit!

Friend, I don't know if you see the thread here: *God was changing our direction*—and it led Shirley and me into a future neither of us anticipated (and weren't even sure we wanted).

Not Just Music

Trying to skim through the next sixty frantic, miraculous years of our journey—which landed us in adventures in many fields of music, book publishing, sports, evangelism, and more—won't be easy, but I'll try. Please know I don't share this to brag; I just realize many readers may not know who I am; in fact, it occurs to me that many of you weren't even born when I was a "teen idol," movie star, and host of my own national TV show ALL AT THE SAME TIME, and you may be scratching your head and wondering how all that could have been.

Well, I'll try to give you a snapshot of me, my family, and my career so that you'll have some idea of who I am, if you don't already.

Record-Breaking Recording Career

Let's start with music.

Since my "debut" at age thirteen on the stage of the local movie theater, *I've recorded more songs than any artist in history.* That's more than my buddy, Frank Sinatra, who recorded 1,500 songs and made classics of most of them in his forty-five-year career. And it's even more than my singing idol, Bing Crosby, who made almost 2,000 songs his own!

I've recorded more than 2,300 songs, in six genres—pop, country, R&B, heavy metal (yes, you read that right), movie themes, gospel, and jazz. I even recorded two *a cappella* albums with college choruses. I hold a record of having songs on the Billboard singles charts for 220 consecutive weeks, and I had forty-one chart hits in the 1950s—one more than my fellow Tennessean, Elvis Presley.

I met this guy named Elvis Presley on October 22, 1955, backstage at a Cleveland, Ohio, sock hop that was hosted by the nation's number-one DJ, Bill Randle, at WERE-AM radio. I had recorded my third million-selling record since March of that year, and was the headliner for the show that night. Randle had brought Elvis up from Shreveport, Louisiana, where the twenty-one-year-old newcomer had been appearing regularly on the Louisiana Hayride radio show as a "rockabilly" singer.

Our last meeting, Memphis International Airport, July 1977—one month before his death

We met backstage, we two Tennessee boys, and shook hands. Elvis seemed shy and a little nervous. He went onstage and lip-synced his only record to that point, a bluegrass country song, "Blue Moon of Kentucky." I could tell he excited the kids with his looks, but not with the song he was mouthing the words to. He got a nice round of applause and left the stage. I followed, and got all the teen screams that night…and when I came off stage, Elvis was gone.

When Elvis made a hit the following February with "Heartbreak Hotel," the statistics show I already had six million-selling singles, two of them being number ones—in eleven months. Sounds impossible, of course, but two of the records were double-sided hits, with both the A and B sides selling over a million each!

LP I released of commercial jazz versions of Elvis' biggest hits

From then on, through the 1950s, Elvis and I became friends though rivals, matching each other hit for hit on the Billboard singles charts. As the decade ended, I had one more chart hit than he did. But thank God for that eleven-month head start!

Greeted by Queen Elizabeth, Command Performance, Palladium, London, 1962

While I was still in college at Columbia University in 1957, married with three kids (so far), several hit records, and a couple of hit movies, I performed at a Royal Command Performance at the Palladium Theater in London. I wasn't long out of Nashville— still wet behind the ears— and I was understandably nervous about performing for the Queen and the Royal Family.

I was told to watch Her Royal Highness while I was singing, because if she applauded ever so politely, so would the audience, which was always influenced by her reaction. After I sang my hit version of Fats Domino's "Ain't That a Shame" (of all things), I saw her and Princess Margaret applauding vigorously—so the audience did, too.

Boy, was I relieved! But I stood in line after the performance to be greeted by the Queen, and when she complimented my performance, I embarrassed myself by stammering, "Thank you, Your Highness—uh, I'm glad you're here."

In England. Where did I expect the Queen to be? Cleveland?

Acting

As I mentioned earlier, it wasn't just all about the singing for me; I've also made a number of movies along the way. I started acting when I was twenty-two (a few months before Elvis did), with *Bernadine* at Twentieth Century Fox, the first teen musical, and I followed by costarring with Shirley Jones in *April Love*, a warm, young-love story with music. I wound up in the Top Ten box office ratings as a "movie star" before I really knew it was happening. I moved my family to Beverly Hills, where I made more successful films during a seven-year deal with Twentieth Century Fox, including a couple of "cult classics"—Rodgers and Hammerstein's *State Fair* with Ann-Margret and Jules Verne's *Journey to the Center of the Earth* with James Mason.

With Shirley Jones in 1957 film, *April Love*

Settling in as an accepted film actor, I branched out into drama and comedy roles, shooting in England, Austria, and Ireland—then back to New York City, where I filmed *The Cross and the Switchblade*, portraying David Wilkerson, a dynamic street minister and founder of Teen Challenge, the most effective drug rehabilitation and rescue organization ever.

Even in the last three years, I've played significant roles in three faith-based family films—*God's Not Dead 2*; *A Cowgirl's Story*, and *Miracle in the Valley*—that have proved successful in theaters…and in people's lives. And, believe it or not, I'm still at it, with another film scheduled to begin shooting six weeks from the time of this writing!

I had a lead role in the *God's Not Dead 2* film.

Sports Enthusiast

I mentioned earlier that I was involved with all kinds of sports in high school; my love for athletics followed me into adulthood, and in 1967 I helped found the American Basketball Association (ABA) and *owned the Oakland Oaks team,* which won the championship in 1969 with Rick Barry and other future NBA stars and great coaches.

Entrepreneurial Endeavors

I've always had a knack for recognizing successful business opportunities, so in the early '60s, I purchased an Arizona radio station and helped start Orange County, California's, only TV station, KDOC-TV. Both did quite handsomely. Then, just a few years ago, I made the biggest deal in the history of the ABC network program, *Shark Tank*, for the American rights to the Air Car, invented by Guy Negre of France, who owns more than fifty patents in Formula One racing. (Still working on that one, but you'll probably ride in one someday!) Business and investing were sidelines, of course, but they intrigued me, and I was successful there, too.

In Ireland filming a movie; won 440 relay for USA

Making the biggest deal in *Shark Tank* history ($5 million)

Philanthropy and Mission-Minded Giving

Shirley and I always believed that from "those to whom much is given, much is asked," and we've prayerfully sought opportunities to share our blessings of our money, our talents, and our time. Along that line, we endowed the Boone Center for the Family at Pepperdine University in Malibu, California, where I've been chairman of the advisory board for more than thirty years. The program features a curriculum that teaches young students how to build moral relationships, for full scholastic credit, to prepare for marriage and family. No other college has such a course, but we're sharing it with other universities.

Shirley and I presenting Pepperdine $3 million for the Boone Center for the Family

We also, with a small circle of like-minded friends and family, started Mercy Corps in our home, as Shirley's empathetically tearful response to the Cambodian food crisis and the Pol Pot-created concentration camps. Amazingly, our little dynamic organization got food and clothing to thousands of refugees imprisoned against the Thai border in 1979. Today, thanks largely to the impassioned and highly effective work of our son-in-law, Dan O'Neill, Mercy Corps is now *a half-billion-dollar-a-year nonprofit organization* that, alongside other organizations like the Red Cross and Samaritan's Purse, rushes humanitarian aid to those suffering in virtually every catastrophe around the globe.

And, like many entertainers, I've participated in and hosted many other good charities, including hosting the Easter Seals Telethon for eighteen years. Helping to raise more than six million dollars to provide support and services for thousands of disabled children made me feel I was fulfilling some of my earliest goals in life.

Though dear Shirley went to heaven ahead of me in January of 2019, I'm still singing, acting, writing, and playing basketball and tennis with my younger buddy, Ed Lubin (he's only eighty-two; I'm eighty-six) every weekend.

I just can't quit—and why should I?

Playing tennis every Saturday at age eighty-six

Bestselling Books and Widely Published Articles

Then there is writing. (I was an English major, after all; writing is kind of my "thing.")

I've written more than 250 columns for World Net Daily and Newsmax (yes, I am a conservative, but I love a lot of liberals) and I've authored fifteen books, two of which sold more than a million copies each (that was in hardcover; millions more were sold in paperback). I wrote the first one, *Twixt Twelve and Twenty*, which offers solid advice for teens, while I was twenty-two and still in college at Columbia, becoming a father to four daughters before I graduated at age twenty-three (with considerable help from my wife Shirley, of course).

And then there's this book, *IF,* which brings us back to our original question:

Who am I to write a book like this?

Equally important, I want to ask: *Who are you?*

My Most Important Project to Date: IT'S ALL ABOUT YOU

Though we haven't met, I know this much: You're an eternal soul, not just a body with eyes and ears. I hope you realize that when your body wears out and dies, you… YOU…your mind and memories, your internal feelings, your developed personality…YOU…reading this right now, will live on.

You will not cease to exist. Oh no. The YOU I'm communicating with right now will exist forever. The real question, then, is in what form and where will you exist for all eternity?

That's the biggest question, and it's the reason I feel more passion—urgency—about this book than I have about any of the others I've written. It's even more important to you and to me than who and where we are right now.

See, friend, I'm a realist. I know my life, blessed as it surely has been, will soon be over. I'm feeling compelled to reach out to you—who, I'm thinking, are probably younger than I am, coming up in a different society than I have, and whose life has been bombarded with more media than mine has ever been.

I'm thinking you're busy, you work hard, and you may not have taken time to consider the most important choice we all make in our lifetimes. I know the feeling. I've at times found myself, in my own experience over many years, so occupied by addressing my own temporary issues that I was spending too little, if any, time addressing the big "**IF**"—the one that has *everlasting consequences* and that confronts every one of us, without exception.

The message in this book springs from great concern for others—some who are in my own family and among my close friends, but also for many others who are still bound by daily needs to the exclusion of even being aware of *the final and eternal choice looming directly ahead for us all*…a choice not one of us can avoid.

So now, in my remaining days, I've made and renewed my decision…made my personal choice…to my great relief and joy.

Friend, it's a yes-or-no, up-or-down choice, and anyone can…and will…make it!

In fact—please listen: Though you may not realize it, *you're making your choice, the choice that will determine where you will spend eternity,* ***right now, each minute, every day.***

Part II

Three Questions

chapter three

Question 1: How Do I Know There's a God?

From the beginning of recorded time, countless "intellectual" people have tried every way they can think of to deny and reject God's existence.

But for me, personally, answering this first question in my quest for truth in the matter of my faith didn't take me long at all: *I see evidence of God's existence and benevolence everywhere around and within us.* I just look around at the world—at the heavens, the stars, the mountains, and all the surrounding physical beauty. I see the perfection of creation as we've always known it from the beginning of time, and view all of that as rock-solid evidence that would convince any panel of rational people that this didn't all just "happen."

Somebody, some incredible Somebody, *did this*!

"The heavens declare the glory of God, and the firmament shows His handiwork" (Psalm 19:1). Whomever God may be, He created all we can see or feel. There never has been and never will be any other cogent explanation for what was obviously *created.*

The eminent and profound Jewish scholar Paul wrote in Romans 1:19 and 20 (NASB):

> That which is known about God is evident *within them*. For since the creation of the world His invisible attributes, His eternal power and divine nature, have been clearly seen, being understood through what has been made, *so that they are without excuse*! (Emphasis added)

Again, I could see that it didn't just "happen."

And that was that.

GOD IS.

I didn't need to be a scientist to figure that out. But I have since consulted some of the best experts in theology and science. Will you accept statements from a couple of pretty good scientists named Albert Einstein and Stephen Hawking? How about Charles Darwin, the "Father of Evolution" himself?

Charles Darwin

Darwin and his "theory" of evolution (that's all he meant it to be—a *theory*) shook scientific thought. Most folks—maybe even you—took Darwin's theory to mean that he was an atheist. However, in his last days, Darwin is reported to have *confessed his firm belief in God.*[2]

In fact, during his last days of life, when he was confined to his bed and could no longer attend the local church where he was a member, Darwin's Christian friends are said to have stood outside his opened window and sang hymns to soothe his soul, till his dying day.[3]

What can we learn from this?

I'll tell you what I see. It's one thing for a scientist to look at the whole, impersonal universe and theorize on how it might have come together in some random, "scientific" way. But it's another thing for that same man, when his life on this "impersonal" planet is coming to a close, to yearn for some assurance that he's not about to die and simply vanish into the "Great Unknown" as if he never existed. That life force in him—his very soul—*knew he was not a meaningless accident,* and he wanted to fall into the arms of the One who meant for him to be.

I love knowing that the "Father of Evolution," Charles Darwin, "evolved" from being a tired, old scientist to taking on a new, heavenly body as he drew his last breath, because he had placed his faith in Jesus and accepted Him as his Savior.

Stephen Hawking and Albert Einstein

Stephen Hawking, the genius physicist from Great Britain who wrote *A Brief History of Time*, couldn't quite bring himself to say specifically that there must be a God in explaining the existence of the staggeringly majestic known universe. But, he did say, "The odds against a universe like ours emerging out of something like 'the big bang' are enormous." Further, he has said, "I think clearly there are 'religious implications' whenever you start to discuss the origins of the universe.... *There must be religious overtones.* But I think most scientists *prefer to shy away from the religious side of it.*"

This is along the lines of what genius Albert Einstein said: "My comprehension of God comes from the deeply felt conviction of *a superior intelligence that reveals itself in the knowable world.*" The physicist who developed the theory of relativity said that!

He later stated, "My religiosity consists of a humble admiration of the *infinitely superior spirit* that reveals itself in the little that we can comprehend about the knowable world."[4] In addition, he said, "Everyone who is seriously involved in the pursuit of science becomes convinced that 'a spirit is manifest' in the laws of the universe—*a spirit vastly superior to that of man.*"

Okay, guys, you're intelligent; you can see where the dots lead, you can add vast numbers and construct convoluted theories few can understand. So, what's the logical conclusion? Where did all this—*all of us*—come from?

WHY CAN'T THESE SCIENTISTS PRONOUNCE *G-O-D*—GOD?!

The obvious just won't do...but why?

I know why.

When explaining the universe, scientists such as Hawking start with the accepted notion of random, mechanistic origins, and then they explain all evidence in terms of that model. You see? They've made up their minds—so they try in vain to build a possible explanation, no matter how "unscientific" it may sound.

So...in my quest for my own rational answers, I took these genius scientists' hesitant but positive acknowledgment as my own.

Dear reader, please see this: If the most brilliant minds of this or any other time have openly come to the conclusion that there must be God—even though they don't want to investigate, proclaim His existence, or say His Name—should you or I bet our eternity that they're wrong?

This "superior spirit," this "superior intelligence," is a PERSON!

There was—is—a God. There has to be, scientifically!

GOD IS.

Quite simply, there is no other explanation for who we are…how we got here…and who can take us to Himself when this life ends.

chapter four

Question 2: What About the Bible?

Firmly convinced of God's existence because of what I just shared with you in the previous chapter (as well as by further research, which I'm sharing with you in appendix B), it was time to tackle my next question:

What about the Bible—is it the divine, inspired Word of God?

I didn't know what writings informed the monks I described earlier, but I did already know a lot about the Holy Bible. Not only had my parents, siblings, and I studied the Bible when I was growing up in Nashville, but I had also taken four years of Latin in high school and *a course on New Testament Greek* in my freshman year of college. (At the time, I thought, as I shared earlier, that I would likely become a teacher/preacher like my teachers in the Christian school.

I wanted to read *koine* ["street"] Greek, the language into which the New Testament was originally translated from Hebrew, so that I might solve some doctrinal issues by going back to the original languages.)

That's how serious I was—and still am—about the Bible.

Again, it didn't take long in my personal search to recognize with absolute certainty the compelling evidence for the Bible *in the Bible itself.* Think about it: Each of the sixty-six books of the Bible we hold in our hands today was originally written by one of more than thirty authors over a period of five thousand years. It is an accurate account of known historical fact, it contains scientific truths (many of which were even unknown to the writers themselves), and declares prophecies about coming events and world-shaping changes.

In other words, the Bible itself *proves itself* over and over.

Shaping Lives and Guiding Actions for Millennia

The *external* evidence that this hallowed collection of books changed the world forever is *incontrovertible.* Not only has it dated the modern calendar, but it has become the best-selling book in the world, changing people, their lives, and their behavior as the most revered, influential, and counted-on book in human history. **It has declared the very definitions of "right and wrong"** and established the earthly, kingdom-shaking foundations of liberty and personal freedom.

No other "religious" guidebook has ever come close to having the Bible's influence or reach. That alone puts it at the top of the list of any list of books that have become essentials on any bookshelf, including *Webster's Dictionary*, *Encyclopedia Britannica*, Rand McNally maps, *Strong's Concordance*, and *The Joy of Cooking*.

But the sales figures don't come close to explaining the uniqueness of the Bible. It's what's *inside* the Good Book that counts. The interior proofs in the Bible lead to only one conclusion: It is the living, inspired, divine Word of God. There simply is no other book like it in the world.

Here's just a smattering of those proofs for now (if you'd like to dig a little deeper, see appendix B).[5]

Proven Record of Prophecy Fulfilled

You've probably noticed that the Bible is long. Very long.

I'm not referring to the number of pages (around twelve hundred, depending on the version) or the word count (almost eight hundred thousand, give or take, again depending on the version)—though it's the all-time champion even in those ways. No, I'm referring to its number of years of existence and prominence. As I said, it was written by more than thirty authors, most of whom never even knew each other. For that matter, few of them knew much, if anything, about what the others had written, because the books of the

Bible were written over a time span of about five thousand years. *And in most cases, the authors never lived near each other and had no way to reconcile their writings if they'd wanted to. They just wrote what they themselves knew.*

Incredibly, many of the authors (prophets) foretold issues and events that were later recorded from the eyewitness accounts of later writers—many times, hundreds of years later. The eyewitness accounts include details establishing that the prophecies were fulfilled *exactly as prophesied, down to minute details, sometimes with names and dates.* Time after time, those foretellings were recorded in one century and fulfilled to the most precise detail centuries later, such as the accounts and descriptions of cataclysmic deeds of God, like the worldwide Flood of Noah's time (Genesis 6–9) and the four hundred years of Israel's Egyptian captivity and subsequent forty-year wilderness wanderings before being led to take the land of Canaan (Genesis14:13–17 and Joshua 11:16–23).

All of these things took place just as the Lord had promised, and they're authenticated and confirmed by secular history and archeology.

This isn't fiction; these are historic, secularly recorded facts.

One of the most profound examples of biblical prophecy being fulfilled is seen in the history of Israel. After the nation's leader, Moses, had led the often-rebellious people of Israel through the wilderness and right up to the borders of the Promised Land, he addressed the millions before him, saying that God had told him he was about to die. Moses said (I'll paraphrase), "After I'm gone, and after all God has done for you, which is more than He's done for any people who ever lived before, *you will rebel and turn away from Him. You will be cursed and taken into captivity. Eventually, HE will bring back the faithful and plant them again in this land, with His word written in their hearts and not just on the parchments you've known and disregarded*" (see Deuteronomy 18:15–31:27).

Hundreds of years later, the Israelites *were* taken into Babylonian captivity and enslaved again for seventy years. Then, just as Moses foretold, they were brought back to Jerusalem, where their temple was rebuilt and their lives were restored.

But yet again, they proved unfaithful as a nation and were later taken over by the Romans. All of their precious buildings, including Solomon's magnificent Temple, were destroyed, and the Jews were dispersed all over the world, virtually vanishing as a nation.

Israel's story was over…

…or so it seemed.

That is, it was over until 1948, when the nation was reborn, *precisely as prophesied by the legendary prophet Isaiah*, when he himself was about to be taken into Babylonian captivity with his people. Read for yourself Isaiah 66:6–11, in which the old man, looking far into the future, was shown how his beloved Israel would literally disappear from the world—and then be restored almost four thousand years later. He asked, "Shall a nation be born in a day?" The answer is "Yes, it shall!"—**as it was on May 14, 1948, when President Harry Truman declared the United States would support Israel as a nation again!**

IN ONE DAY, ISRAEL WAS REBORN—two thousand years after she ceased to exist and was dispersed around the world, and four thousand years after Isaiah and Ezekiel prophesied she would be born again…in a day (Isaiah 66:8 and Ezekiel 37:21–22)! What other "book" in history can claim such accurate fulfillment of prophecy?

Since then, millions of Jewish people have been returning to the Promised Land from all over the world, AND Jerusalem is once again its capital!

Though the Jewish people are yet again having to defend their God-promised right to the land, we know, on the authority of His Holy Word, that they will never be driven out again or deprived of what the Lord promised Abraham, Isaac, and Jacob: that the land "would be their eternal possession."

Please tell me you see what I'm showing you: Almighty God is in charge! He governs what happens in all the nations and every part of the world. When He tells us in His Holy Word what He's going to do, we can count on the fact that

He'll do it! Since everything in Scripture is written and promised and available to all of us, we're absolute fools to ignore, disregard, or try to resist any of it!

Countless other internal proofs provide us with solid evidence that the Bible is inspired (Holy Spirit-breathed) by its real author, God, but the history and contemporary events taking place in and around Israel are something we're seeing lived out right before our eyes—a five-thousand-year-old story foretold, experienced, and fulfilled, just as proclaimed in the grand old Book.

Scientific Evidence for Biblical Events (God Knew We'd Need Them)

From physics to archaeology, the world of science time and again lends astonishing support to the validity of biblical people, places, beliefs, and events.

For example, were you aware that Noah's ark is sitting on top of Mount Ararat in Turkey right now? It has been photographed from above and substantiated in our time!

I have friends who have taken expeditions up that rugged, almost unapproachable peak, into the always ice-covered area toward the top of Ararat. It's very rare for anybody to reach or attempt to reach the upper levels of the mountain, because the weather is always bad and the climb is extremely dangerous—and why go there?

Well, whaddya know? That old Bible actually states *specifically* in Genesis 8:4: "Then the Ark rested in the seventh month, the seventeenth day of the month, on the mountains of Ararat"!

Friend, your Bible, the Genesis account, was written at least five thousand years ago, almost certainly by Moses, who was an extremely educated and brilliant man, raised in the family of the Pharaoh of Egypt. Who even knew there was a mountain named Ararat? And what difference would it make down through the centuries, anyway?

God knew.

And he knew how prone we'd be to dismiss His truth and His account of His purposes on this earth, among the humans He created in His own image.

My friend, John Anderson, and some fellow scientific believers set out for Turkey, got the permissions to make the dangerous trek up the rugged, foreboding mountain, and came back with their lives (barely), some hacked-off pieces of wood preserved in the ice, and aerial photographs of "a mysterious boat-like structure that [surprise!] matched the exact dimensions of Noah's Ark as described in Genesis!"

The explorers took the wood pieces to carbon dating experts, who opined that the wood, fairly well preserved, was likely too new (by a thousand or so years) to be from the ark.

But since then, the whole "science" of carbon dating

has been called into question by other experts and declared unreliable for dating the wood.

Question: **IF** that is NOT the Ark on Mount Ararat, how do we explain the photographic *evidence that it must be some OTHER huge boat on top of that mountain*...and how did that one get there? Any ideas?

Psalm 14:1: "The fool has said in his heart, 'There is no God.'"

By biblical definition, then, the scientist who denies God is a *fool.*

He's not even a reliable scientist.

The bottom line is this: Neither you nor anyone else has a real excuse for not believing the Bible is the greatest book in the world...and it, too, is *created by the living God.* (Again, if you would like to dig into this topic a little deeper, please see appendix B on page 213.)

chapter five

Question 3: What About Jesus?

"What then shall I do with Jesus who is called Christ [Messiah]?"

~PONTIUS PILATE, MATTHEW 27:22

Back to my intent to confirm or erase my long-held faith, based on hard evidence, I next wanted to find out more about Jesus. Convinced beyond any doubt of the first two conclusions of my faith journey—1) God IS, and 2) the Bible is His infallible, loving, saving Word to mankind—I set out to answer my final question:

Who is Jesus? Is He the Son of God, or a myth…a folk legend?

How can I know?

Now…friend, please stay with me. You'll never read anything more important than the next few paragraphs!

Eyewitness Accounts

Who was—*is*—this most famous person in recorded history? He's certainly not the subject of a myth or a legend; there is more eyewitness, factual information recorded about this young Jewish man than about any of the world rulers or prominent people of His time!

Even modern-day Orthodox Jewish historians agree that a famous person (though they're not sure of His professed divinity) emerged from Nazareth in the first century AD whom thousands of fellow Jews believed to be the promised Messiah. Their own perusals of secular histories of that time have confirmed unanimously that He was reputed to have performed miraculous feats, including raising the dead. They also confirmed that He eventually was condemned to crucifixion by the Jewish leaders for fear He might foment some kind of rebellion by his followers against the Roman occupation…likely bringing grief on the already oppressed nation of Israel.

More Questions

As I've shared, I could see that there is no contradiction to the fact that Jesus WAS—that He in fact existed. But that just opened the door to many more questions.

WHO was He? Was He the Son of the Living God, as He claimed both privately to His followers and eventually openly to His accusers and executers? And **IF** He was the Son of God, why on earth would He have submitted to earthly rejection and grisly death by crucifixion?

These are the logical questions I asked—for myself, and now, for you.

Finding compelling evidence for Jesus Christ's life, ministry, death, and resurrection didn't take me long, at that time. I knew where to look, and I soon came to rational and proven substantiation of what I'd taken by faith as a young boy.

I'm eager to lay it all out for you, too (see appendix B for even more evidence). I don't believe you'll ever question His existence—or purpose for coming—again.

But for now, suffice to say that, if we're satisfied that the Bible is divinely inspired and therefore is God's very Word—His expressed love and will for us all—we *can't miss Jesus*!

He is the hero, the champion, the *focus* of the whole Book!

Jesus: The WORD of the Word

See, I already knew that from Genesis' first words, "In the beginning, God created," to some of Revelation's closing words: "Surely I am coming quickly. Amen. Even so, come,

Lord Jesus!" the Holy Book concentrates on God's creation of human beings in His own image, and emphasizes His tireless and longsuffering patience with us throughout the centuries (which, as we learn in Psalm 90:4 and 2 Peter 3:8, are just *moments* to Him).

And, not coincidentally, most scholars agree: Every book from Genesis through Revelation was written by Jews. We Gentiles didn't get in on it till after Jesus was crucified and rose again.

We read of GOD'S exasperation with our frailties and selfishness, His sacrifice of His own Son as the final offering for our sins on a Roman cross, and His inviolable promise to take to Himself all who will accept and believe in Him.

If you read straight through the Bible, start to finish, as I have almost forty times now—you can't miss the unbroken story line: *Jesus had to come from heaven to rescue fallen humankind from ourselves.* Over and over through the ages, the human race has proved itself unable to become fit for eternal habitation with our Creator God.

That led inevitably to the astonishing statement in John 3:16:

> For God so loved the world that He gave His only begotten Son, that whoever believes in Him should not perish but have everlasting life.

AND I SAW IT!

I saw who Jesus is and why He had to come!

We couldn't save ourselves! It's like a blind man trying to find his way through the train station to reach his home: Unless someone who can see and knows the way can help him, he'll never make it! Never!

I then knew why Jesus had to proclaim "I am the way, the truth and the life. No one comes to the Father except through me" (John 14:6). He *came from heaven—He* knew the way home—and *He* wants to take us there!

I knew I could never get there on my own. My Greek studies in college would never gain me access to heaven. I'd never be good enough on my own to find—or earn—my way to heaven. Those dear monks in Thailand couldn't get to heaven by burning themselves alive. Instead, I had to knowingly put my faith, my belief, in the One who'd been there and who wanted to take me by the hand and take me there!

Let's get specific.

Notice that I did not say I needed to "believe *about* Him," as in accepting the fact that Jesus existed in history. No, John 3:16 specifically says "believes *in* Him," as in accepting that He is the Savior of every man, woman, and child who receives Him into their hearts and lives, and who proclaims Him and their relationship with Him intimately and personally.

Please see this for yourself: No one else in human history ever could promise you, personally, eternal life!

When I was just a little boy, and into my teens, my friends and I sang this song: "Jesus loves me, this I know, for the Bible tells me so… Yes, Jesus loves me, yes, Jesus loves me. Yes, Jesus loves me, the Bible tells me so."

Maybe you heard or sang this song yourself when you were growing up. Its words are true! Praise the Lord…they're true!

In fact, I'll let the Gospel writer John tell you right now, better than I can myself. This is the very beginning of his book, the first chapter of John:

> In the beginning the Word already existed.
> The Word was with God,
> and the Word was God.
> He existed in the beginning with God.
> God created everything through Him,
> and nothing was created except through him.
> The Word gave life to everything that was created,
> And His life brought light to everyone….
> He came into the very world He created, but the world didn't recognize Him. He came to His own people—and even they rejected Him. But to all who believed and accepted Him, He gave the right to become children of God. They are reborn—not with a physical birth resulting from

human passion or plan, but a birth that comes from God.
So the Word became human [*flesh*] and made His home among us. (John 1:1–4, 10–14, NLT; emphasis added)

My friend, dear reader—these two-thousand-year-old very words about the very Word made flesh, Jesus, the Son of the Living God—have literally brought life and light to untold millions of people just like you and me to this very moment, as you read.

They changed my life when I was barely thirteen, and they continue to dramatically affect and change me to this very day!

Back to the Garden

Let me take you to a place I've visited many times. It's a beautiful garden called Gethsemane, where there are many very old olive trees dating back to the first century AD. It's a holy, shadowed grove, preserved for its significance for more than twenty centuries.

Let's go back in time, to just after midnight in the spring of the year, following a solemn Passover Seder in Jerusalem. Many devout Jews from many nations had come to commemorate God's deliverance of His people from four hundred years of slavery in Egypt.

But while most slept, in the still of the moonlit night, a small group of men came quietly into this garden…to pray. They were led by a Man named Jesus. A tremendous commotion had been made over Him when He had ridden down from the Mount of Olives *on a donkey,* while huge throngs of men, women, and children had waved palm fronds and exclaimed, "Blessed is the King who comes *in the name of the Lord!* Peace in heaven and glory in the highest!"

This display of adoration had infuriated the Jewish leaders. They couldn't stand that one of their own, from His humble birth in lowly Bethlehem, would allow Himself to be celebrated this way. *They either weren't aware of Zechariah 9:9 or didn't want to know that their own exalted prophet had foretold the coming of Messiah in just that incredibly humble way!*

So those leaders devised a plot, with the help of one of Jesus' own disciples (Judas), to have Him killed—and hopefully right away, before His popularity could increase even more. They were afraid He'd bring the wrath of Rome down on all of Israel.

Jesus knew this.

He knew that His very name, *Jehoshua* ("Jesus"), means "Jehovah is Salvation." He knew He had been commissioned by His Father—God—to take on human form and bring eternal salvation to all who would receive Him—even the Jews and Romans who were ready to kill Him. He came to this garden with three of His closest disciples to pray in preparation for the horror He knew was about to happen to Him—God in human form.

Please, reader, use your imagination and try to see this.

Let's tiptoe in the shadows over to where Jesus is on His knees, hands lifted toward heaven, praying to His Father in such agony of spirit that great drops of blood ooze from His pores. We hear: "FATHER…Father, if it is your will…take this cup[6] away from me. Nevertheless, not my will, but yours…be done."

Then we see Him rise, hoping to pray with His disciples but finding that they're asleep. Just then, a multitude of priests and Roman soldiers led by Jesus' disciple, Judas, tramps through the garden to arrest Jesus and take Him to a trial that will lead to His crucifixion.

As the disciples run away and the soldiers and priests fade back into the night, you and I are alone, still in the garden, trying to digest and comprehend what we've just seen and heard.

Who was this Man?

Most folks on the street were very excited about Him. They'd heard of—and some had seen——mighty miracles He had performed by His touch, His words, His presence: vision restored to blind eyes, hearing restored to deaf ears, withered arms straightened, fatal illnesses like leprosy healed.

Even a number of men and women, girls and boys had been raised from the dead! The city of Jerusalem still reverberated with excitement about the recent time when Jesus had called Lazarus from the tomb where he'd lain dead for four days!

Who wouldn't have been excited! Wouldn't you?

So why? WHY? Why didn't Jesus slip back to the Galilee, to Capernaum, even out into the wilderness? He had avoided arrest before—passed right through one crowd that intended to throw Him off a cliff outside His home town of Nazareth—*when He confided in them that He was the one Isaiah prophesied would come as Messiah.*

Right there that night, in the garden, He told His disciples He could pray to His Father, and His Father would "provide [Him] with more than twelve legions of angels!" (Matthew 26:53). That's seventy-two thousand angels! He had said this in front of those who were arresting Him in the garden—and He could have called forth those angels—but He didn't.

But get this, and read it for yourself in Matthew 26: Just when the priests and soldiers approached Jesus in their armor, swords drawn, Judas identified Him with a betrayal kiss on the cheek. Jesus calmly asked, "Who do you seek?" One soldier answered, "Jesus of Nazareth." (See John 18:5.)

Jesus answered, "I AM He."

Jesus: The I AM

The armed soldiers fell backward to the ground, armor clattering, swords falling from their hands.

They were powerless and embarrassed.

I read this many times without realizing their astonished reactions were because Jesus gave them the same answer God had given Moses from the burning bush when Moses had asked, "Who can I tell Pharaoh is ordering him to let My people go?"

God's answer to Moses had been "I AM…I AM that I AM. Tell him that."[7]

So, when Jesus spoke those profound words to describe His identity to the soldiers in the garden those many hundreds of years later, His statement knocked the soldiers flat! They "fell under the power of that proclamation of Who Jesus is"! I AM! (see Luke 22:70).

Peter, then, emboldened by seeing the soldiers overcome, grabbed his sword and lopped off the ear of one of the priest's servants. Jesus sternly commanded that Peter put away his sword, then He touched the severed ear, and it was healed instantly (Luke 22:49–50).

Those soldiers and temple guards could never say they didn't know who was meekly allowing Himself to be taken away to a rigged trial. But His disciples, knowing who He was, couldn't fathom why He didn't just lead them away and out of the garden. The question was hanging in the cool, dark, night air.

Then Jesus gave the answer to WHY, WHY…WHY?

Quietly, in the stunned silence, He said: "How then could the Scriptures be fulfilled, that it must happen thus?"

Though nobody understood what He was saying in that mind-blowing moment, He said it *knowing that one day you and I would hear* it and understand that God Himself, His Father, planned this from the beginning of time and foretold it in Scripture. It had to happen exactly as it did! The very Son of God then walked voluntarily out of the garden toward His trial and crucifixion.

Do you see what I'm showing you? Not exactly? Well, I'll come back to this scene in a few minutes, but let me give you more mundane, less emotional reasons.

Friend, *we date our calendar from the birth of this man named Jesus*! And your eternal birthdate is set from the day you establish your belief in who this God/Man was…and is.

There's so much more proof that Jesus was—is—the very Son of God. Not only do we see it in the ways He fulfilled prophecy, but in the fact that details of His life were carefully recorded by people who had known Him and had seen him.

Jesus: Fulfillment of Prophecy

No one who considers all the Scriptures concerning the coming Messiah in Isaiah 53 and in the books of Zechariah, Micah, and Malachi can rationally deny that these all point to Jesus—even to the fact that the Messiah would be born in Bethlehem!

For example, toward the end of the Old Testament, just before the Gospel of Matthew begins the narrative of Jesus' life, the prophet Micah speaks explicitly of the expected and coming Messiah:

> But you, *Bethlehem* Ephrathah,
> Though you are little among the thousands of
> Judah,
> Yet out of you shall come forth to Me the One to be
> Ruler in Israel,
> Whose goings forth are from of old,
> From everlasting. (Micah 5:2–4)

How about Zechariah, the greatly respected prophet whose book many scholars believe should have been placed at the end of the Old Testament and just before the beginning of the New Testament? Specifically foretelling the coming of Messiah, he wrote:

> Rejoice greatly, O daughter of Zion!
> Shout, O daughter of Jerusalem!

> Behold, your King is coming to you:
> He is just, and having Salvation [Hebrew Jeshua], lowly and riding on a donkey, a colt, the foal of a donkey [as Jesus did, coming down from the Mount of Olives into Jerusalem while huge crowds cheered]. (Zechariah 9:9)

Just a little later, Zechariah added:

> And I will pour on the house of David and on the inhabitants of Jerusalem the Spirit of grace and supplication; **then they will look on me whom they pierced. Yes, they will mourn for him as one mourns for his only son—and grieve for him as one grieves for a firstborn.** (Zechariah 12:10, emphasis added)

That simply couldn't describe anybody but Jesus!

Friend, there's so much more…many prophetic pictures of the Jesus who would come in their near future.

Jesus: Seen, Heard, and Referenced in History

Further strengthening the evidence that Jesus is who He said He is, we see that His existence and ministry are mentioned not just in the Bible itself, but also in extrabiblical sources. One of the more notable is from the first-century historian Josephus in his book, *Antiquities*, which traces the history of the Jews from the dawn of recorded time through the late first century. Josephus wrote:

> At this time there appeared Jesus, a wise man, for he was a doer of startling deeds, a teacher of people who received the truth with pleasure. He gained a following both among many Jews and among many of Greek origin. And when Pilate, because of accusations made by the leading man among us, condemned him to the cross, those who had loved him previously did not cease to do so. And up until this very day, the tribe of Christians, named after him, has not died out.[8]

Josephus was a Jew who didn't convert to Christianity… he just recorded what he knew to be true. That makes his account all the more remarkable.

Jesus: Resurrected Savior

But dear friend and reader—nothing convinces me that Jesus truly is the Son of God more than the scene in the dark Garden of Gethsemane you and I witnessed at the beginning of this chapter. Not even a crazed maniac would knowingly submit to the torture, the humiliation, and degradation that Jesus knew He was about to suffer—when He obviously could have just disappeared and avoided it all.

But just a short time earlier, in the Upper Room, He had told His disciples:

> The Father loves me because I sacrifice my life so I may take it back again. No one can take my life from

me. I sacrifice it voluntarily, for this is what my Father has commanded. (John 10:17, NLT)

Who else on God's green earth would ever have been willing to do what this God/Man did for us?

Only JESUS.

And what **makes** Him our Savior rather than simply a martyr for his "religion" is the fact that, after he laid down His life for us, ***He arose.***

How can we know this?

For starters, *we have eyewitness accounts recorded in the four Gospels,* as well as from nonbiblical references by Josephus, about the excitement building among early Christians after the resurrection. It was Josephus who wrote that Jesus' brother, James—a post-resurrection convert who became leader of the Jerusalem church—suffered a violent death for his beliefs. This nonbiblical reference by a respected early historian is significant. Why? It offers additional corroboration that Jesus' followers were willing to die for the One they saw resurrected…including His own brother who hadn't initially believed in His divinity…

…until He came back from the dead.

Then there are the other apostles. "In forty days, these men who were afraid to suffer with their leader were transformed into bold and fearless witnesses," D. James Kennedy, a noted pastor, evangelist, and author said. "Most of the apostles were eventually condemned to a martyr's death. To believe that the apostles would suffer persecution and terrible death for what they knew to be a lie *is beyond credible belief.*"

Finally, there is the most famous of the apostles—Paul. It was his face-to-face encounter with the risen Christ on the road to Damascus that led to his conversion (read Acts 9).

Paul was formerly known as Saul of Tarsus, a Pharisee who hated and persecuted Christians. What did he have to gain by becoming a devout follower of the One he had considered a dangerous imposter? He knew his conversion would lead to certain death—and he wound up paying for his faith with the ultimate sacrifice. Why would he willingly die if he hadn't witnessed the resurrected Jesus?

And even further verification: In the book of 1 Corinthians 15:5–8, Paul writes that after the resurrection, Jesus "appeared to Peter, and then to the twelve [disciples]. After that, *he appeared to more than five hundred of the brothers at the same time, most of whom are still living, though some have fallen asleep*. Then he appeared to James, then to all the apostles. *And last of all he appeared to me also*."

The reference to the five hundred eyewitnesses, most of whom are "still living," is not contradicted in any way in any nonbiblical literature of the time; neither are any of the other references to Jesus appearing to other witnesses.

Lee Strobel, an attorney and author of *The Case for Christ*, said:

> If you were to call each one of the witnesses to a court of law to be cross-examined for just fifteen minutes each, and you went around the clock without a break, it would take...129 straight hours of eyewitness testimony. Who could possibly walk away unconvinced?[9]

Christ was simply, emphatically, and undeniably **God, come to earth**; His love transcends anything we could ever know.

So...how can I know? Because of all of the above, of course—but more than anything else, my visit with you to the Garden of Gethsemane, where we see this remarkable, miraculous, uniquely gifted God/Man submit to arrest and all the coming abuse, rejection, and horrible crucifixion—*which He knew fully well was coming*, and which He could have sublimely sidestepped in a second—is the ultimate proof to me.

He left heaven, from His place beside of His Father, to do exactly what He did. *He gave* His very life, his body, and His blood, to rescue you and me from the eternal death we all face...without Him.

He could have *called down angels*. He could have *created whole new worlds and countless other races of obedient, grateful, fantastic people*...**IF** He had chosen to.

But instead, *He chose you*, and me, and every single one who will receive the salvation He purchased on the cross.

What's your choice?

Part III

If

chapter six

Every Blessing Comes with an "IF"

Now...let's turn our attention to YOU.

I believe I've proved to you that God is real, omnipotent, and all-knowing—and that, amazingly, He actually *loves us,* His created beings, so much that He wants to spend eternity with us!

I believe I've also established that the Bible is undoubtedly a miraculous, inspired Book. It's a Holy Book that God breathed...inspired...through many devout men over many centuries, and it's one that can be trusted to tell us nothing but truth—scientifically, historically, and spiritually.

Therefore, I believe you shouldn't have any doubt that Jesus is the Son of God, *literally God in the flesh,* who lived among us as a Man, tempted and tried in all ways—yet without sinning, not even once.

Now what? What are **you** supposed to do with all of this?

I'm so glad you asked! I hoped and prayed you would. That proves you are a thoughtful, rational person who wants to make sound choices—and who wants to make good use of supremely valuable knowledge.

Before I answer that, though, I want to tell you something you've probably never heard before, something that may surprise or even shock you, as it did me when I first realized it—just recently:

EVERY BLESSING OF GOD COMES WITH AN "IF."

Think about that for a minute. Let it sink in.

It's a little jarring, isn't it? Do I mean that God takes back gifts He has given us? Are His gifts and blessings conditional? Does He hand us something with one hand—then take it away with the other?

Is relationship with God like a game of chance? Is the deck stacked somehow, with a ledger being kept by a bookkeeper in the back room? Is it like rigged slot machines or tables with cards and dice where the plays always favor the house?

The Bible says no one is righteous (Psalm 14:3 and Romans 3:10); we're all sinners (Romans 2:23); and if we "think" we are in good standing with God, we should "take heed lest [we] fall" (1 Corinthians 10:12). Do you have to buy a ticket to get into the game? Is there a referee waiting and watching, ready to blow a whistle and bench you if you step over the line or break a rule?

None of the above. Far, far from it.

I'm on ticklish ground here, and I know it. But there are so many who think about God and what He wants for us in those trivial, misinformed ways. As they consider whether they want Him in their lives, they don't like the "odds."

IF they feel they probably can't measure up and meet His demands, they opt out, deciding not to get in the game at all. I understand. I've had some of those feelings and reticence myself.

I was raised in a church background where the prevalent doctrine was an incomplete understanding of Philippians 2:12: "Work out your own salvation with fear and trembling." To us, that meant we should try our very best to please God and "earn" our salvation by good works, selflessness, "doing unto others as we wanted others to do for us," and generally trying to be as near to perfect as possible. Only on judgment day would we know whether we had "made it."

That's a pretty tough lifelong assignment, right? It's not very attractive to people in this tempting, corrupt, "grab whatcha can," seductive world we're living in.

The trouble is, we never seemed to understand the very next verse, Philippians 2:13: "For it is GOD, *who works in you both to will and to do for His good pleasure*" (emphasis added).

How does He do that?

I'LL TELL YOU: His Spirit comes into you and me and causes us to actually *want* to do His will, and gives us the inner power to do it for His good pleasure—and for our present and ultimate salvation.

In effect, He does it *for* and *through* us.

But that involves a big "IF"—and we'll come back to that in just a bit.

Right now, I'm a little ahead of myself, so let's go back to the beginning. And by that, I mean let's go back to the very beginning, when God started this whole thing going and uttered the first big "IF."

The First Big "IF"

"In the beginning, God created the heavens and the earth" are the first words in the Bible, the Holy Book honored and believed by all Jews and Christians. Scholars presume the Creation account was written by Moses, probably while he was wandering by God's decree in the wilderness of Sinai for forty years. That's when Moses had plenty of time, and God wanted the leader of His chosen people, the Israelites, to let all future generations know how we got here and what His purpose was for us on this one, relatively small globe in the giant cosmos.

Creating the world and everything in it appears to have

been an incredible experiment, one only a Creator God could conceive of or execute.

What was His purpose? Was it to see if He could create a perfect world and human beings created in His image to populate it, and to see if He could raise them like a Father, to love Him and want to be like Him?

Apparently...He was looking for friends. And family.

He wasn't looking for robots, and He wasn't even looking for more angels. He already had plenty of those. Instead, He desired *children* who would want to be like Him and who would choose to be His kids!

See? Until then, everything He had done was perfect, because *He* was perfect. He could *speak* what He wanted—and it would come to be. But evidently, He wanted children who would have a lot of the same creative abilities and sensibilities they saw in Him. And even with all that power and knowledge and perfect surroundings—and even though they would be given free will so they weren't robots who *could* only do His will—they would *choose* to love, honor, and obey Him...

...*because they wanted to*!

What a beautiful, original, stupendous dream! Only God could have dreamed it.

It started well—but it didn't go the way He hoped.

God created the first man and woman, perfect in every way, and set them in a beautiful, bountiful garden called Eden. He gave them everything they could possibly want, including each other, walking around unclothed in a perfect, warm climate (the first nudist colony?).

Wanting to see **IF** they really loved Him and wanted to be like Him, *He gave them the first* "**IF.**"

Spending time with them each day, showing them how everything worked and how they could tend their garden, He only gave them one prohibition. He did this to see if they would be obedient children and want to please Him.

"See that lush, elegant tree there in the center of the garden?" He asked. "I call it the tree of the knowledge of good and evil."[10]

His instructions were simple: "You don't need to know what that means, because I've got all that covered. Perhaps in time, when we know each other better, I'll explain. But for now, it's not meant for you. Don't touch it or eat its fruit. Just leave it alone."

Then He warned what would happen **IF** they disobeyed.

"Oh, and just in case you're tempted to eat the fruit, don't. **IF...IF** you do, you'll die. Just believe what I tell you. Don't do it."

Well, as you likely already knew, a terrible, fallen angel named Satan (who wasn't a slimy, scary snake...yet) cozied up to impressionable Eve, gained her confidence, and then introduced a second huge, seductive "**IF.**"

"Oh come on, Eve, God didn't mean that," the evil one said. "He knows that **IF** you eat that delicious fruit, you'll be as wise as He is! Won't that be great? Go on, take a bite, you'll love it."

So Eve was tricked into eating the fruit, while Adam watched. When he saw that she didn't drop dead after she took that first bite, he said, "Let me have some of that."

I don't know whether we can imagine how deeply hurt and disappointed God must have been about this. All of His creative work, His plans for a population of untold thousands or millions who would love and obey Him and be His family on earth, were shot down right in the beginning. God can't break His own word. Why should He? So, rather than wipe the whole thing out and start over, He instituted plan B—and sent the first couple out into an uncharted world to "work out their own salvation, with fear and trembling" (Philippians 2:12).

Some people think this story is a fable, an allegory, a fairy tale.

It's not.

The Bible says it really happened, just that way, and Moses (who, remember, was the one whom God had instructed to write about it) was a lot closer to that event than any naysayers today. Jesus refers to this account as well; numerous scriptural passages relate Him referring to Adam, Eve, and their descendants.

In fact, Jesus is referred to as the "second Adam" (1 Corinthians 15:45), restoring the possibility of eternal life to all who believe Him…just as the first Adam's *lack of belief* and obedience doomed the whole human race—including you and me.

THERE WAS NO SECOND CHANCE.

DO IT—DIE.

Several thousand years later, Jesus, the Second Adam, reversed the fatal sentence when He said: "**RECEIVE ME—LIVE.**"

Friend, we've just looked deeply into the first "**IF**"**—and we've seen the awful consequences of choosing the wrong side of it.** What's that got to do with you or me? Look, dear reader…you and I are paying the consequences ourselves, because *we're both under the same death sentence as the first Adam.*

That's why this little word, "**IF**," is so big.

chapter seven

"IF": Small Word, Big Power

Two letters: *I-F.* How important can that tiny word be?

"IF only—." "IF you hadn't—." "IF I could just—." Huge matters hang on what that little word says and on the world-changing circumstances and events that sometimes follow it.

IF Noah...Hadn't Listened to God

Talk about world-changing! Let's revisit the account of Noah and the Flood we first talked about in the foreword of this book.

Again, it's a familiar story for many, so you'll probably remember that, in Noah's day, the Lord saw how wicked people had become. He was sorry he had ever made them and put them on the earth.

It broke His heart.

So, He decided to wipe every living thing—all the people, the large animals that thunder across the fields, the small animals that scurry along the ground, and even the birds that soar through the sky—from the earth.

But…

BUT…

A man named Noah found favor with the Lord. Noah was a good, God-honoring, obedient man, the only blameless person living on earth at the time. God led him to build the ark in which he and his family—eight people in all—along with a portion of the world's living creatures, were able to ride out and survive the massive Flood that wiped out all other life on earth.

IF…

IF…Noah hadn't remained faithful in following God and trying to be like Him, all life on earth would have been destroyed.

See how important that little word can be?

IF it wasn't for Noah and his family, you and I wouldn't be communicating right now—we probably wouldn't exist.

IF Abraham...Hadn't Listened and Obeyed

Now let's jump forward in biblical history four hundred-plus years to consider Abraham. As we read in Genesis 19, Abraham was talking with the Lord outside his tent in the wilderness of Judea, and the Lord told him He was going to check on the sinful, corrupt city of Sodom with the obvious intent of utterly destroying it and everyone in it. Abraham nervously tried to "negotiate" with God.

"You won't destroy the righteous with the wicked, will you Lord?" Abraham asked.

The Lord answered with—you guessed it—an "**IF**":

"**IF**...I find fifty righteous people in Sodom," the Lord said, "I will spare the entire city for their sake."

Abraham only knew of his nephew Lot and his wife and two daughters living in Sodom, so he dared to "negotiate" further with the Lord, finally getting Him to reply with another "**IF**":

"**IF** I find ten righteous people, I will not destroy the city for their sake."

The *trouble is, the Lord didn't find even ten righteous folks in Sodom.* The other side of this "**IF**" was the annihilation, the fiery, absolute destruction of Sodom and its sister city, Gomorrah, and every living being in those cities—except, by God's grace, Lot and his two daughters.

Why didn't I mention Lot's wife just now? Well, because she ignored a big "**IF.**"

You see, the angel that was rescuing Lot's family on the morning of the searing catastrophe had warned them *not to look back* while they were rushing frantically up the hillside to escape the town. The angel said, in essence, "**IF** you look back, you will be consumed." Common sense says that we can read that as, "**IF** you don't look back, you will be kept safe." But Lot's wife was too curious (like Mother Eve), so she turned and looked back.

On the spot, she became a pillar of salt—an inanimate, mineral statue—and her grieving family had to continue without her.

See why I'm urging us to pay attention to the word "**IF**"?

"IF" Moses…

Many generations after the days of Lot, near the end of the Israelites' four hundred years of captivity and slavery in Egypt, God responded to the cries of His people by arranging for a babe named Moses to be taken into Pharaoh's house and family and to be raised as a son of the king. The baby's very Egyptian name means "called out"—and, indeed, this boy would be singled out by God and used by Him to lead two and a half million Jews out of slavery and into the Promised Land. Before that Exodus was accomplished under Moses' leadership, the Lord sent twelve plagues upon Egypt, because Pharaoh kept refusing to "let God's people go."

The night before Pharaoh finally obeyed God's command to free the Jews, the Lord, through Moses, instructed His people to take a lamb or a goat into each household. They were to kill the animal, save its blood, and roast and eat part of the meat along with unleavened bread (no time for baking fresh bread). Then they were instructed to use the blood to make a mark over the doorpost of their family's dwelling.

And they were to pack quickly, so they would be ready to go.

God said He would send an angel of death through the whole land at midnight to strike all of the firstborn males in Egypt, "both man and beast: and *against all the gods of Egypt…I AM THE LORD*" (Exodus 12:12, emphasis added).

Further, the Lord said the blood would "be a sign for you in the houses where you are. And when [read "**IF**"] I see the blood, I will pass over you; and the plague shall not be on you when I strike the land of Egypt" (Exodus 12:13).

There is no record of any of the Jewish people failing to do what God commanded. They had seen His power miraculously displayed on their behalf. Hurriedly, and in terror, they obeyed.

What about you? Would you have opted to take the other side of that "IF" to see whether God was really going to do what He promised?

Do you understand what I'm trying to help you see?

Let's go just a little farther.

Later, after Moses had led the people out of Egypt through the Red Sea, which miraculously parted to expose a dry-land passageway, he went up on Mount Sinai to receive the Ten Commandments *written by the finger of God* on two tablets of stone.

But that's not all the instructions He gave Moses for the people to obey.

If you take the time to read Exodus, Numbers, Leviticus, and Deuteronomy—as I have many times and find fascinating—you'll find a detailed, meticulous, and demanding list of rules God now expected His people, His rescued family, to follow.

Why did God impose on His now-liberated people these incredibly time-consuming requirements and observations?

Because He knew them.

Their human nature included a tendency to shirk "odious" obligations and seek their own ways, forgetting all about the God who had set them free.

He wanted them to be reminded frequently and through planned feasts and worship events that they were His family on the earth, His chosen ones.

And because He knew them so well, after He "laid down the law" through Moses, He gave them one of the most serious "**IFs**" yet:

> [IF] you walk in My statutes and keep My commandments and perform them, then I will give you rain in its season, the land shall yield its produce, and the trees of the field shall yield their fruit. (Leviticus 26:3–4)

In many of the verses that follow, God promises every conceivable blessing for the Israelites' obedience: He would provide them with plenty of good food; an abundance of provisions, peace, and protection from their many enemies; and victories in battle. God seemed to be assuring them that He would provide them with every good thing they could think of and even more:

> I will walk among you and be your God, and you shall be My people. I am the Lord your God, who brought you out of the land of Egypt, that you should not be their slaves! (Leviticus 26:12–13)

BUT…here comes yet another "**IF**" that is the promised result of disobedience to all those instructions:

> **[IF]** you do not obey Me, and do not observe all these commandments.
>
> and **IF** you despise My statutes, or **IF** your soul abhors My judgments, so that you do not perform all My commandments, but break My covenant,
>
> **I also will do this to you:**
>
> I will even appoint terror over you, wasting disease and fever which shall consume the eyes and cause sorrow of heart....
>
> I will set My face against you, and you shall be defeated by your enemies.
>
> Those who hate you shall reign over you, and you shall flee when no one pursues you. (Leviticus 26:14–17, emphasis added)

My friend, please read it for yourself: This is just the beginning of a long list of terrible consequences *God promised to bring on the people of Israel* **IF** they disobeyed, disregarded, or discounted His commands by walking away from Him and turning to other "gods" who would perhaps be less demanding.

Sadly, that's just what most of the Israelites eventually did. After they made a start and established the pattern of living life in God's way, within just a very few years, many had drifted into outright rebellion and idol worship. Though God had passionately wanted to bless them and had given them ample opportunity to grow into a people who would show the world what God wanted to do for us all, **His chosen nation fell apart.**

The people and their leaders completely deserted God's will, disobeying and denying Him in every way—and He dissolved them completely.

That was three thousand years ago—and only in 1948 did Israel become a nation again.

God had said, at the end of the "blessings and curses" passage, in effect, "The land will be left desolate, and all my people disbursed around the world, and there will be no nation, as I had hoped. *But in a distant time, I will remember the land and not cast them away, nor shall I abhor them to utterly destroy them and break My covenant with them—for I am the Lord their God.*"

Those promises to Israel are being carried out right now before our eyes! I myself was just recently in Israel as part of a celebratory concert on its seventieth anniversary as a nation in the modern era.

I hope you're seeing this. It's all true, good and horrible, and historically accurate. Every word.

It's important for you to know that *the God of our day hasn't changed from the God of ancient Israel, not one iota.* He's the same God who chose Israel as His own, who made them the envy of the known world—and planned with His Son to bring a Messiah, a Savior, into this corrupted and dying world to grant eternal life with Him through His people.

HE didn't forsake them.

HE keeps His promises—for blessings...and curses.

"IF My People..."

In the oft-quoted 2 Chronicles 7:14—which includes probably **the best-known "IF" in the Bible,** to Christians and Jews alike—God promises His people (not just the Jews) that "**IF** my people who are called by my name will humble themselves, and pray and seek My face, and turn from their wicked ways, then I will hear from heaven, and will forgive their sin, and HEAL THEIR LAND" (emphasis added).

That verse sounds so good that we quote it often today, appropriating those words to ourselves, as if we are somehow heirs to those national blessings. However, many of us don't take the time or go to the trouble to read the next few verses, in which God says that **IF** His people forsake Him and go after false gods, He will DESTROY THE VERY TEMPLE THEY ARE DEDICATING AND WIPE OUT THEIR NATION.

Were they listening? Are you and I listening?

Here's a startling revelation I received as I was writing this. In my daily reading of the Bible, I found myself in the book of Jeremiah, which was written 350 years after the Chronicles passage we just read was recorded. In Jeremiah

7:14, the prophet himself quotes the same God by inspiration of the same Holy Spirit. Jeremiah said the Lord had reached His limit with the rebellion and abandonment of His will by His chosen people, and declared:

> So just as I destroyed Shiloh, I will now destroy the Temple that bears my name, this people that you trust in for help, this place that I gave to you and your ancestors! And I will send you out of my sight into exile, just as I did your relatives, the people of Israel....
>
> I will pour out my terrible fury on this place. Its people, animals, trees, and crops will be consumed by the unquenchable fire of my anger. (Jeremiah 7:14, 20, NLT)

And that's exactly what history records that *He did.* You can read the accounts for yourself.

When the people did what God asked, He made them the greatest nation in the known world at the time. But—the huge "**IF**"—when they fell away and abandoned Him, *they virtually vanished from the face of the earth,* only to have God bring them back from all over the globe today to have another opportunity, two thousand years later, to fulfill what He promised Abraham, Isaac, and Jacob. In spite of our disastrous failures, He doesn't forget His promises to those who will still—today—obey Him.

God Never Changes

I want you and anyone who will listen to realize: YOU DON'T MESS WITH GOD! He said emphatically about Himself, "I DO NOT CHANGE!"

He was and will always be the GOD we're reading about right here. It's the very reason I'm compelled to write this!

You can't wish Him away or *think you can dismiss His will* and purpose for you, for your life. He's still building his forever family, which will only be composed of the select, relatively few, who (like Noah and his family) obediently, deeply, and faithfully *want* to be His children.

We've looked at these examples of how people throughout biblical history have responded to the Lord's "**IFs**"—from Adam and Eve, Noah, and Abraham and Lot to His chosen people, Israel. Now, let's move to the One who says, in effect, "I AM the big '**IF**'."

chapter eight

Jesus' Life

I am the way, the truth, and the life.
No one comes to the Father but by me.

–JOHN 14:6

Who in this world could say such an audacious thing? What human being would dare to present Himself as the one and only Savior of every man, woman, and child in this world?

Jesus.

He also said many other things that drove many of those who heard Him into furious, murderous rage.

Why would He say that, *knowing He would be put to death for it*? Because that's why He came—not just as a human being, born like we all are, the product of love between a man and woman—but as a God/Man, born of the love of a Father for every woman, man, and child who accepts and receives Him.

My friend, we've come a very long way to this point, and I think you still might be thinking: *Wait, Pat, you're just a guy who's telling me all this and expecting me to just give up all my doubts and difficulty in believing that this Man, Jesus, is the Son of God and the Savior of the world. I just don't know if I can believe that.*

Look, I know it's hard to put our finite minds around this. It doesn't seem possible, or even conceivable, to the modern, natural sensibilities. But we're endeavoring to move into *super*natural possibility, aren't we?

Jesus' Birth

It *was conceivable*, naturally and supernaturally, in the womb of innocent young Mary, when the Holy Spirit of God created the embryo of His own divine Son and the angel told her, "Do not be afraid, Mary, for you have found favor with God—and behold, *you will conceive in your womb and bring forth a Son, and shall call His name Jesus*" (Luke 1:30–31).

It was conceivable then…so we must conceive of it now. And—mystery of mysteries—*Jesus will be conceived in us*!

Do you know what the name "Jesus" means? It's used

often as an epithet and even a curse word, but those who utter it in those ways have no idea what they're actually saying. I'm so grateful to author/minister Carl Gallups, who, in his fantastic recent book, *The Rabbi Who Found Messiah*,[12] reveals that Jesus' Hebrew name, *Jehoshua*, means "Jehovah is salvation." Now please get this, take it in, and understand; it's vital to your eternal destiny. Jesus, from His very birth, was called *Jeshua*, the short version of *Jehoshua*, which literally always meant "salvation"—for, as the angel continued in his announcement to the young Mary, her coming Son would "save His people from their sins."

In Hebrew, the name is *Yeshua*...which literally means "salvation." So what Mary heard the angel say in Hebrew was that she "shall call His name 'salvation,' or 'God saves'."

God saves!

Jesus' very name, from the beginning, *proved His identity and His mission on earth.* His parents knew, as impossible as it was to comprehend, that their baby boy in the manger was meant to be the prophesied Savior of all mankind.

His name said so!

Can you picture the young boy running around in Nazareth with His brothers and the other kids, hearing them calling "Hey, Salvation! Wait, God Saves! Slow down, wait for us!" And upon hearing that, Mary would remember the old prophet Simeon—whom an angel had told he wouldn't die before he had "seen the Lord's Messiah"—taking the eight-day-old baby in his arms, blessing God, and saying the following:

> Lord, now You are letting Your servant depart in peace…
> For my eyes have seen Your salvation [Jesus]
> Which You have prepared before the face of all peoples,
> *A light to bring revelation to the Gentiles,*
> And the glory of Your people Israel. (Luke 2:25–35, emphasis added)

Surely God had planned for Mary to be the first one to tell the young boy how He had been born under such unprecedented circumstances—yet born for this time and in this place for God's own purposes, which were beyond her understanding.

But Jesus would have to read the Scriptures for Himself, listen for the voice of His Father even in His youngest years, and try to understand what all this meant—and what would be required of Him.

Sure enough, before He was twelve years old, He astounded the older Jewish teachers with His knowledge of the Scriptures and explained to His parents when they came to take Him home, "Didn't you know I have to be about my Father's business?" (see Luke 2:41–50).

You see, Jesus shared the very DNA not only of His earthly

mother, but of *His Heavenly Father, the God of all creation!* Undoubtedly, Jesus prayed often and fervently, asking for wisdom and understanding of the reason He had been born with this mission, this unfathomable task that had already been spelled out to Simeon, and even what the angels had meant when they sang at His birth, telling the shepherds He would bring peace to the peoples of earth.

No one but God could tell Him, because no one else on earth could conceive of it.

Picture this: Jesus, as an otherwise normal young boy, knew the Scriptures that foretold of His birth and many others about the expected Messiah who would come. Then His Mom told Him, "*Son, God told me you're the One!*"—but she didn't always express it with pride and excitement. Rather, she had an air of grave foreboding, both for Him and herself.

Even Joseph, Jesus' earthly "daddy," had been instructed by an angel to take Mary and the baby Jesus away by night to Egypt to escape the terrible slaughter orchestrated by Herod the next day: Every male child age two or younger would be killed in an effort to *eradicate the one who might be the Messiah*!

Obviously, Jesus and His parents discovered early on that Jesus being God's Son and the promised Messiah would be a terribly *costly, dangerous,* and *eventually fatal* mission. His future was transcendentally majestic on one hand and ominously tragic on the other. Try to imagine the cost of this commission by the Lord Most High.

Yes, Mary's soul would be pierced to its core—not her body, but her soul, like yours and mine.

How ironic—or sublimely poetic—that, as He grew into manhood, Jesus worked with wood alongside Joseph, a *carpenter*. The very hands that fashioned useful articles and furnishings from wood, in a not-too-distant day, *would be nailed to a wooden cross* as He fulfilled His earthly destiny. When that day came, He'd be fashioning eternal salvation for those who would receive it, as His very name promised, on a wooden cross.

Yes, that's the One who so audaciously proclaimed to be "the way, the truth and the Life"—the Man named "Salvation."

JESUS. *JESHUA.*

No book in the world other than the Holy Bible has ever conveyed a story like this—rife with human, intimate details; conversations; inner thoughts; and hidden purposes foretold and fulfilled to the nth degree! No other but a Holy God could declare what He would surely do in one century, then accomplish it exactly as foretold in another—and later give writers the whole, multilayered story and facts to record—for us who are alive on the earth *today*.

Isaiah, perhaps the most respected of the Hebrew prophets, described in great detail the Messiah who would come.[13] He quoted the Lord:

> I have a plan for the whole earth—a hand of judgment *upon all the nations.*
>
> The Lord of Heaven's Armies has spoken—who can change His plans?
>
> When his hand is raised, who can stop him? (Isaiah 14:26–27, NLT; emphasis added)

Earlier, the prophet had relayed this to King Ahaz:

> Listen well, you royal family of David....
>
> Isn't it enough to exhaust human patience? Must you exhaust the patience of my God as well? All right then, the Lord Himself will give you the sign. *Look! The virgin will conceive a child! She will give birth to a son—and will call him Immanuel* (which means "*God is with us*"). (Isaiah 7:13–14, NLT; emphasis added)

Some try to interpret Isaiah's words not as "virgin," but rather as "young girl." But the prophet was offering this *as a sign of the coming Messiah.* How convincing would it be for simply a "young girl" to give birth? *The fact that she was a virgin, of course, is what made this birth miraculous...and a "sign."*

Isaiah's prophecy was spoken and recorded *seven hundred years before* Mary became pregnant. After the young virgin shared the news of the coming birth with Joseph, an angel appeared to the hurt and perplexed husband-to-be, who was considering having her "put away," as the Law allowed.

Consider what the angel said:

> Joseph, son of David...do not be afraid to take Mary as your wife. For the child within her was conceived by the Holy Spirit. And she will have a Son, and you are to name Him Jesus [in Hebrew, "Salvation": "the Lord Saves"!]—for HE will save His people from their sins. (Matthew 1:20–23, NLT; emphasis added)

The Gospel writer Matthew goes on with his account:

> All of this occurred to fulfil the Lord's message through His prophet Isaiah:
>
> Look! The virgin will conceive a child!
> She will give birth to a son,
> and they will call Him Immanuel,
> which means "God is with us."
>
> (Matthw 1:22–23, NLT)

If you're concerned about the difference between "Immanuel" and "Jeshua," "Jesus," and "salvation," don't be. They all mean the same thing.

Isaiah gave even more specifics in the prophecy about the coming Messiah:

> The people who walk in darkness will see a great light.
> For those who live in a land of deep darkness, a light will shine....

For a child is born to us,
a son is given to us.
The government will rest on His shoulders.
And HE will be called:
Wonderful Counselor, Mighty God, Everlasting
Father, Prince of Peace.
His government and its peace will never end.
He will rule with fairness and justice from the throne
of His ancestor David for all eternity.
The passionate commitment of the Lord of Heaven's
Armies
Will make this happen!
(Isaiah 9:2, 6–7, NLT)

Has there ever been another person in the world's history about whom these things could have been said? Mohammed? Confucius? Buddha?

Show me. And then tell me how that might have worked out.

For two thousand years now, nations (such as Great Britain, Israel, and America) that have based their laws and rules of society on Judeo-Christian principles, including the Ten Commandments and the caring instructions Jesus gave in the Sermon on the Mount, *have led the world and been the envy of all the other nations, whatever their religions may have been.*

Jesus' Ministry

At age thirty, Jesus' ministry—of being God on earth, in human form—began.

He walked into the Jordan River, where His cousin John was creating a national stir, calling fellow Jews to repent of their sinful nature and get ready for the Messiah who was about to appear. John was baptizing people, "burying" them in water to symbolically wash away their sins.

And suddenly there was Jesus.

John, the preacher, knowing the Messiah was coming and wanting to recognize Him, was told by God, "When you see the Holy Spirit descending like a dove on a man—you'll know He is the Messiah" (see John 1:33, 34).

And as John looked at his cousin coming to be baptized, he sensed that Jesus might be...possibly *was*...the One. Hadn't He been called "Salvation" (Jeshua) His whole life? Had He ever been known to commit a sin?

When John hesitated to baptize Jesus as He asked, Jesus commanded, "Baptize me. I must do this to fulfill all righteousness" (Matthew 3:14, 15).

Even though Jesus had never sinned, He knew He was to obey His Father's will. So John, too, obeyed, and baptized his cousin. As Jesus came up out of the water, dripping, the *heavens split open,* the *Holy Spirit descended* on Jesus in the form of a dove, and a *voice from heaven thundered,* "You are my dearly loved Son. and you bring me great joy"! (Matthew 3:17).

Would you like to have been there among the hundreds who witnessed this remarkable event? Would there ever have been any doubt that this Jesus truly was the promised Messiah? GOD'S VOICE FROM HEAVEN ANOINTED HIS SON!

Drink that in, my friend; visualize it.

In your mind, stand there on the bank of the Jordan River and absorb that scene and all it meant to mankind—to you—and God's purposes in finally gathering a forever family to Himself.

But wait! The same Holy Spirit that just unmistakably identified Jesus then led Him out into the Judean wilderness (I've been there, and it is the most lonesome and deserted place you'll ever see) to fast for forty days before meeting Satan face to face to be tempted most dangerously.

Earlier, at His baptism, Jesus had heard the commendation in the voice of God Himself. Then He heard the cunning, sly, seductive voice of the one who *had led Adam and Eve into the sin that represented the Fall of the entire human race!*

Weak as Jesus was physically because of His lack of food and water, He was strengthened by the Holy Spirit and His own sinless life, and He faced Satan down with Scripture—God's Word that had been woven into the very fabric of His mind and heart.

He won the first climactic fight of His earthly ministry!

Of course, the story of Jesus' ministry doesn't end there. In fact, it's only the beginning of the greatest story ever told. I can't tell it all here, of course, but please stay with me just a bit more.

As soon as Jesus went back into Galilee after His time in the desert, filled with the Holy Spirit's power, He was asked to speak in area synagogues. It was standing room only everywhere he preached, as you might imagine. His travels eventually led to His hometown of Nazareth, where, as a local hero, He was handed the Scriptures to read aloud.

Get this now: As the crowd hushed, He opened the scroll and read:

> The Spirit of the Lord is upon me
> For he has anointed me to bring Good News to the poor.
> He has sent me to proclaim that captives will be released,
> That the blind will see,
> that the oppressed will be set free,
> and that the time of the Lord's favor has come.
> (Isaiah 61:1–2)

Everyone recognized these words from the prophet Isaiah as describing the Messiah who would come—someday. Then, in the silence, Jesus rolled up the scroll and said, in effect:

"This Scripture you've read and heard for seven hundred years has been fulfilled this very day…

…it's about me."

Were the people thrilled and excited?

No!

"How can this be?" they demanded. "Isn't this Joseph's son? He's just our 'home boy.' This is sacrilege!" They got so riled up and angry that they tried to drag Jesus to a cliff outside town and throw Him over the edge of it to His death. But God protected Him; Jesus just slipped through the crowd and disappeared.

My reason for retelling these things here is to underscore the age-old truth: *Lots of people just don't want to hear about Jesus*, and they don't intend to ever accept Him as God's Son, "the way, the truth, and the life."

Millions of people who have never even explored the possibility, never cared to know Him or why He could so dramatically say it, simply refuse to consider the **only Man in human history** who boldly said, "**I'll personally take you to heaven IF…IF…*IF* you'll let me**"!

Well, fasten your seatbelt.

You may not like to hear even more astounding, shocking, and ominous things He said that may affect your eternal destiny.

chapter nine

Jesus' Words

We've looked at many of the historical accounts *about* Jesus. Now we're going to listen directly *to* Jesus, God's beloved Son, the longed-for Messiah, the One whose very name is "Salvation," "God saves."

Again, He is the One spoken of in the familiar John 3:16:

> For God so loved the world that HE gave His only begotten Son, that whoever believes in Him shall not perish but have everlasting life.

Sounds so loving, so inviting, doesn't it? And it is, my friend; *it is.*

That verse continues:

> He who believes in Him is not condemned…

GOOD! Let's keep going.

BUT [an "IF"?] he who does not believe is condemned already, because he has not believed in the Name of the only begotten Son of God!

Wait a minute!

The verse sounded so good at first, but now it sounds like **IF** I don't believe, I'm already condemned...lost. Forever.

Yes, that's exactly what it says. And it's in red letters... Jesus said it Himself.

Eternal Life Is Costly

At that moment, early in Jesus' already miraculous ministry of healing the sick, giving sight to the blind, and enabling the lame to walk, He was talking at night, alone, to the prominent Jewish leader, Nicodemus.

Jesus used the example that Nick knew well, an account in Scripture about Moses being in the wilderness with the Jews, who had been grumbling and complaining about their circumstances. God had become very angry, and had *brought a killing plague of fiery serpents among them*. Many were dying and screaming for help. When Moses prayed, God told him to lift up a bronze serpent on a tall pole. Anyone who had been bitten and gazed at the raised bronze serpent *would be healed,* the Lord said. And, though thousands died, *those who heard believed, obeyed, and lived.*

Jesus continued to speak with Nicodemus:

> For God did not send His Son into the world to condemn the world, but that the world through Him might be saved....
>
> But he who does not believe is condemned already [like the snake-bitten Jews in the desert], because he has not believed in the name of the only begotten Son of God. [That name? *Jehoshua*...Jehovah is Salvation!] (John 3:17–18)

Suddenly sounds harsh, doesn't it? It's because *it's a life-and-death matter—your life and mine.* It's exactly as if you have a fatal illness and someone has to tell you so that you can find healing.

Only Jesus Can Pay the Price

You see, even God's patience and forbearance have their limits. This thing called eternal life is costly. God wanted to give it to us so much that He was willing, through the ghastly crucifixion and death of His Son, the shedding of His own Son's sinless blood, to pay the unpayable price of our sins, our guilt.

The Bible says that God and His Perfect Son—the physical extension of Himself—agreed before we were even created that this would be necessary, because we, with our free will, self-interest, and outright sinfulness could never come up with the price of our own redemption.

Why?

Because without the shedding of blood, there is no forgiveness of sin (see Leviticus 7:11 and Hebrews 9:12).

Both the Old and New Testaments are in complete agreement—getting forgiveness from God requires somebody's blood!

What? BLOOD? Real blood?

Pat, what are you saying!?

Suddenly, we see how deadly serious this "salvation" thing really is! Throughout human history, God has made it plain that *only the shedding of innocent blood can wash away the guilt of sins*, whatever they may be!

Going back to the Garden of Eden, when Adam and Eve disobeyed the command of God, their perfect *bloodline, their divine DNA,* like an umbilical cord, was severed. **The price of disobeying God always was death…and it still is. Because of their original sin, we all die. It's unavoidable. We all sin, every one of us.**

So God, loving us so much, told Moses, "Don't ever eat blood. You can eat meat, but drain it first; don't eat the blood."

You see, life is in the blood of all things. Life. And only sinless blood can pay the price of sin.

Who has any sinless blood?

I don't—do you?

Stay with me now. God made a covenant with Abraham, Isaac, and Jacob, and then with Moses and the people of Israel, that He would be their God, and they would be His chosen people on the earth:

> Therefore, not even the first covenant was dedicated without blood. For when Moses had spoken every precept to all the people according to His law, he took the blood of calves and goats, with water, scarlet wool and hyssop, and sprinkled both the Book itself and all the people, saying "This is the blood of the covenant which God has commanded you." (Hebrews 9:18–22, NLT)

So…take a deep breath, and thank God, as the Jews did: The Lord wasn't requiring them to each roll up their sleeves and donate their own red blood.

Why?

Because their blood was already soiled and polluted with sin and disobedience, and they knew it. God instituted animal sacrifice—the selection and slaughter of innocent, beautiful animals—to provide pure blood to "wash away" sins. Whew!

The people were relieved, as you must know—but they were getting the message emphatically and repeatedly—*only innocent blood can pay the price for rebellion against God and His will.*

In the book of Hebrews in the New Testament, then, we read about the New Covenant the Lord made with the Jews, the promise Jesus was instituting and **sealing with His own blood**...again:

> Almost all things are purified with blood...and without the shedding of blood THERE IS NO REMISSION. (Hebrews 9:12–14, emphasis added)

Whose blood does this refer to—yours? Mine? Who has sinless blood to shed in order to purify, bring *remission... forgiveness...cleansing of sin,* of our *blood guiltiness*?

Only Jesus, the One whose name is "God Saves" "Salvation."

JESUS. JESHUA.

Only His righteous, sinless blood could pay for our sin and reconnect our DNA to a Holy God.

Jesus knew this when He opened the scroll that day in Nazareth, when He was speaking in the synagogue. He knew this when He confronted Satan face to face in the desert. He knew this when He had his late-night talk with Nicodemus.

He knew this from the start.

He knew what our salvation was going to cost Him when He delivered the Sermon on the Mount overlooking the Sea of Galilee.

A Strong Message

I've been to the Sea of Galilee many times, and I read that passage every year. But it didn't hit me until recently how bluntly, how starkly, how "in your face" He spoke to the many people who were hearing *His first major, public sermon.*

His message started with love and blessing—the lovely Beatitudes:

> Blessed (happy) are the poor in spirit...those who mourn...the meek...those who hunger and thirst for righteousness...the merciful...the pure in heart...the peacemakers...
>
> [But wait!]
>
> *Blessed are those who are persecuted for righteousness' sake*...and blessed [happy] are you when they revile and persecute you, and say all kinds of evil against you falsely for My sake....
>
> Rejoice and be exceedingly glad, for great is your reward in heaven, for so they persecuted the prophets who were before you. (Matthew 5:3–11)

Then, He said:

> You can enter God's Kingdom only through the narrow gate. The highway to hell is broad, and its gate is wide for the many who choose that way. But the gateway to life is very narrow and the road is difficult—and only a few ever find it. (Matthew 7:13–14, NLT)

This was Jesus' "closer," the end of *His first sermon*, in which He made it starkly clear that following Him is not a cakewalk. Following Him is difficult, dangerous, and not always fun. It doesn't simply require attending services once a week; it demands great and lasting faith, adherence to God's will and commandments, and a lot of help from our brothers and sisters along the way.

The Lord knew, as He looked out at that huge crowd, that, once they really got the picture of what following Him meant, *a great majority would choose not to do it.* Only a few would take the narrow way—**the only way to eternal life with God.**

Please catch the sober truth of this. These aren't my words; they are the clear, sad, reluctantly spoken words of the Son of God. THIS IS THE BIGGEST, MOST URGENT "**IF**" of all.

Each of us faces a fork in the road: We must decide whether to stroll into the wide, easy way…or to strike out on the narrow, more difficult way.

God wants us to choose the latter. He "is not willing that

any should perish," but that *all should come to repentance* (believe and turn to Him for salvation; see 2 Peter 3:9). He so passionately wants us to make that choice—He so zealously loves us—that "He gave His Only Son, that *whoever believes in Him should not perish*" (John 3:16).

You see, God, through His Beloved Son, offers eternal life to all *who choose Him*!

IF we choose the wide way, the easy way, we are declining that offer.

IF we choose the narrow way, the more difficult way, we are accepting that offer, the one He made for us with great sacrifice to give us never-ending life in the blessing of His care and love.

Do you see this huge "**IF**" looming in front of you?

I made my choice long ago, and it's locked in.

WHAT IS YOUR CHOICE?

chapter ten

Jesus as Judge

Jesus is the Savior, the King, the Messiah, and the One God appointed to execute final judgment.

Yes, I said the word "judgment." No one thinks that's a fun topic, but judgment is coming, as sure as we're born, and we'd best be preparing for it.

What *I* say about this subject isn't worth a hill of beans. What does matter infinitely and eternally is what Jesus says about it from His throne in heaven at the right hand of His Father.

Let me preface this look at Jesus' words about judgment with a true story my dear friend, Harald Bredesen, told me years ago. He was a Dutch Reformed minister, one who always said "yes" to whatever he felt God asked of him. What a man!

As he explains it, he was driving through a small town in Connecticut one day. He was driving a little fast because he was running late, and his mind was on the sermon he was preparing to preach the next morning. Wouldn't you know? A cop stopped him for speeding. Even though Harald wasn't going more than ten miles above the signed limit, the small-town officer insisted on taking him before the judge.

The old judge seemed a little crotchety, and after spending a couple of minutes listening to the cop's story, he turned to Harald and said, "That'll be $150. Pay up now."

Harald never had much money, so he let the judge know he was a minister from a nearby town and had just been trying to get home to preach his sermon in the morning. He hoped that would convince the judge to let him go with a warning. But the judge shook his head no. "The law is the law, Reverend. You of all people should know that. You broke it; you pay the penalty."

Harald wrote a check for the fine and handed it to the judge.

"You're right, Your Honor. I was wrong, and I'll pay the fine. God bless you."

Harald drove home feeling pretty down.

But two days later, he got a letter from the judge.

It read:

> Dear Reverend, I'm the judge; the law says I had to fine you. But it doesn't prohibit me from paying your fine. Here's your $150 back.

Harald knew that through this experience, God was giving him a topic for many more sermons! An honest judge must uphold the law...but it's a rare one indeed who will pay the penalty himself.

That's what I want you to know and concentrate on now: The Judge is coming, and His name is Jesus.

Hell: It's the Real Deal

Jesus said unexpectedly harsh things throughout His earthly ministry. In fact, it might surprise you *just how much He talks about hell*—and about who's going there. Although Jesus is the embodiment of love, there appears to be anger and at least terrible frustration in many of His statements, especially regarding those who dishonor His Father.

For example, in His first sermon, the one we referred to earlier called the Sermon on the Mount (read Matthew 5, 6, and 7), He concludes the section called "The Beatitudes" with this sudden turn:

> You [the throngs listening to Him] are the salt of the earth. But what good is salt **IF** it has lost its flavor? Can you make it salty again? It will be trampled underfoot as *worthless.* (Matthew 5:13, NLT; emphasis added)

Hmm. That doesn't sound so nice.

The next example is extremely important, especially if you're Jewish. (You see, what most Jews and many Christians don't realize is that the whole Bible is Jewish! From the first chapter of Genesis to the last chapter of Revelation, the Bible recounts Jewish history, recorded almost entirely by Jews, about Jews, and for Jews. Almost all of the events described in the Bible take place in the tiny nation of Israel and relate the four-thousand-year saga of how God produced—through the Jews—the Messiah, the One who would offer salvation to the whole world.) Still, in the next verses of His sermon that day, Jesus spoke directly to the Jewish leaders who were certainly in the crowd:

> Don't misunderstand why I have come. I did not come to abolish the law of Moses or the writings of the prophets. No—I came to accomplish their purpose. I tell you the truth, until heaven and earth disappear, **not even the smallest detail of God's law will disappear until its purpose is achieved**. Anyone who obeys God's laws and teaches them will be called great in the Kingdom of Heaven.
>
> But I warn you—[the "**IF**"]—*unless* your righteousness is better than the righteousness of the teachers of religious law and the Pharisees [the self-righteous, super-critical, hypocritical leaders among them], *you will never enter the Kingdom of Heaven*! (Matthew 5:17–20, NLT; emphasis added)

Understand—Jesus is the "new Jew," the One everybody came to see and hear, telling off the religious establishment right to their faces in the audience! Further, He added: "If you curse someone, you are in danger of the fires of hell!"

And He was just warming up!

He didn't let anyone guilty of any wrongdoing off the hook:

> **IF** your eye…causes you to lust, gouge it out and throw it away…**IF** your strong hand causes you to sin, cut it off and throw it away. (Matthew 5:29–30, NLT; emphasis added)

These are very strong images, and some think they're meant as hyperbole. But Jesus concludes with an even more vivid warning:

> It's better for you to lose one part of your body than for your whole body *to be thrown into hell.* (Matthew 5:30, NLT; emphasis added)

There's that hell again. Apparently, Jesus knew firsthand what some liberal theologians today have largely dismissed as a real concern. Jesus warned about hell *as if He knew it really existed.* He was trying right from the start to scare the people He died for, to keep them from going there for eternity.

Included in Matthew chapter 6—still part of the Sermon on the Mount—is the Lord's Prayer, a simple, sublimely sweet, and direct instruction from the Lord on the proper way to pray. In verses 14–15 of the prayer, we read:

> **IF** [there's that word again!] you forgive those who sin against you, your heavenly Father will forgive you. But **IF** you refuse to forgive others, **your Father will not forgive your sins.** (Emphasis added)

Meditate on that for a little bit. Where will you be **IF** God will not, cannot, forgive your sins? Remember Harald's honest judge?

After pronouncing the blessings of His Father on all those who seek the kingdom of God and make a real effort to live righteously, Jesus lays down the hallowed Golden Rule:

> Do unto others as you would have them do unto you. This the essence of all that is taught in the law and the prophets. (Matthew 7:12)
>
> Wonderful, isn't it? Everybody likes that one.
>
> But look at the what comes next:
>
> You can enter God's Kingdom only through the narrow gate! The highway to **HELL** is broad, and its gate is wide for the many who choose that way. But the gateway to life is very narrow and the road is difficult—*and only a few ever find it.* (Matthew 7:13,4, NLT; emphasis added)

Friend, there is a real hell.

It was prepared initially for Satan, fallen angels, and demons who continue to oppose everything God wants done in this world. Satan is real, merciless, and cunning, and he wants to take as many human beings as he can into the pit of eternal fire and punishment. He wants to fool them into rejecting the One named "Jesus," "Salvation," and "God Saves."

This Satan, who is terribly real, is the same creature who deceived Eve and Adam into disobeying God—and who *put you and me under an inescapable death sentence already*! He's already the reason you'll die—now he's determined to plunge you into an eternity with him!

That should badly frighten you.

Fear is a great motivator. In fact, in several places, the Bible declares that the "fear of the Lord is the beginning of wisdom" (see Proverbs 9:10, for example).

I know that's true. IF we have any sense at all, the probability, the very idea, of a real hell should make us very afraid. *Over and over, Jesus warned of the real hell—and of the certainty that a majority of human beings will go there.*

Hell Should "Scare Us Out of Hell"

That truth scared the young Pat Boone—and I'm glad it did.

As I shared earlier, I grew up in a Christian family, thank the Living God. My dad was an architect and builder; my mama was a registered nurse. Both were in very practical professions. My brother, two sisters, and I learned early on about Jesus, His church, and the Bible. It was rather expected that when any of us reached around the age of twelve, we would individually walk down the aisle at church during the invitational song to profess our faith in Jesus and be baptized.

My younger brother, Nick, went down the aisle as soon as he turned twelve. I hadn't decided to do that yet, because I was doing some Bible reading on my own, wanting to understand better what I was doing and why. But just as I turned thirteen, I came across Matthew 10:28, where Jesus had just said:

> Do not fear those who kill the body but cannot kill the soul—but rather *fear Him who is able to destroy both body and soul in hell.*

I knew the "Him" in that verse was Jesus, and I was scared.

But then, just four verses later, I read:

> Therefore whoever confesses me before men, him I will also confess before My Father who is in heaven. But, whoever denies Me before men, him I will also deny before My Father who is in heaven. (vv. 32–33)

A thirteen-year-old kid can understand that.

And I did, joyfully. I understood there was a heaven—and a hell (and I sure didn't want to go *there*!). So, in just a few days, I answered the invitation during the service, walking down the aisle of my church "before men" and confessing my faith in Jesus to secure my eternal salvation. I was baptized immediately, to my parents' delight.

I've just turned eighty-six now, and I'm starting to get really excited about hearing Jesus "confess me" before His Father and the angels, and about embracing my dear wife again, since she got there before me.

I share this because it's an important part of the reason for this book.

I want to "scare the hell out of you." —Or, better, I want to "scare you out of hell." It's real, and the day is coming soon when it will be too late to "confess Jesus" in this life.

Knowing—and Known by—Jesus

We never actually die—did you know that? Oh, these mortal bodies give out and go away, but the real *person, the soul, the spirit,* goes on *forever.*

Isn't that good news?

Well, yes it is…**IF.**

Who decides where that real spirit person goes?

The Judge. The Righteous Judge.

You and I, in our spirit bodies, will appear before the Judge, whose name is Jesus.

That's why I've focused on His words—on what He says, not on what I or any theologian, social manipulator, or false interpreter *hope* He means.

What has Jesus said about that moment in our existence?

Read a preview in John 3:35–36:

> The Father loves His Son and has put everything in His hands. And anyone who believes in God's Son has eternal life. Anyone who does not obey the Son will never experience eternal life but remains under God's angry judgment. (NLT)

Jesus *and* God are the judges? And God is angry?

Maybe, like Harald, you and I might try to use our occasional "goodness," our "religious" upbringing, our fine efforts to help others less fortunate, anything else that seems righteous and selfless—anything to influence the decision in our favor…right?

But back to *Jesus' first sermon*, recorded in Matthew 7:21:

> Not everyone who calls out to me "Lord! Lord!" Will enter the Kingdom of Heaven. Only those who actually do the will of my Father in Heaven will enter.

> On Judgment Day, many will say to me "Lord! Lord! We prophesied in your name and cast out demons in your name and performed many miracles in your name! Doesn't that count?"
>
> But I will reply, "**I never knew you.** Get away from me, you who *break God's laws.*" (Matthew 7:23, emphasis added)

"*I never knew you.*"

WHAT…DOES…THAT……MEAN?

If you're married, or have been…how did you get to "know" your mate? I don't just mean sexually. Knowing someone, really knowing them, involves deep dedication, commitment, selflessness, faithfulness, love, and literally desiring your mate's happiness more than your own. Right?

It means marriage. Vows. Promises and promises kept. Intimacy, giving of "self." Penetration. Conception. New life. Creation…together. Oneness. Sacrifice. "Till death do us part."

You can do a lot of nice things for people, even for people you don't know.

But marriage—*knowing*—means deeper intimacy than you'll ever know or experience with anybody else.

Please read Genesis 4:1, right in the very beginning, just after the first couple was forced to leave the perfect garden that had been created for them. "Now Adam ***knew*** Eve, his wife, and she conceived and bore Cain, and said 'I have acquired a man from the Lord'."

Understand? When Jesus is allowed to enter you spiritually, received by you totally and intimately, a new person is born.

You.

It means giving your life to—and for—someone else.

That's exactly what Jesus meant when He said, "I never KNEW YOU!" In other words, He said:

> I wanted to be married to you; I was completely committed to YOU. I loved you enough to die on a cross for your sins, to save you forever! I've repeatedly referred to the body of believers as MY Bride, each one having openly committed to Me, repenting of sins, saying a VOW of total surrender to Me as Savior, and being baptized and opening completely to My Holy Spirit!
>
> KNOWING ME.
>
> I longed for you to want to know Me—enough to spend the rest of your existence with me. To be married to Me, vows and all—as if you—and I, together, were in a wedding ceremony—"confessing Me before men" so I could "confess you" before My Father—and claim you as my own. But I never mattered that much to you—you were always too concerned with

your own interests, so I never came to KNOW you. Nor did you come to know Me.

My friend, dear reader...we come now to the central point, the whole reason I believe God Himself instructed me to write this book and has brought you to this moment reading it, however that happened.

This is the moment—your side of the biggest "**IF**" of all: the everlasting choice we all must make. Do you really desire to go to heaven and live with your Father God for all eternity?

He wants you—do you want Him?

IF you're convinced and ready to confess your faith in Jesus as the Son of God, believing HE gave Himself willingly to die for the sins you've committed in your life—*asking Him out loud* to forgive and BE your personal Savior, to stay with you the rest of your earthly life, and to eventually admit you to heaven, "confessing you before His Father," saying, "Father, this one is MINE, I KNOW THIS ONE"—then do it.

Do it *right now*!

"Wait!" I hear you asking, "What do you mean? Do I just say it out loud, here where I am?"

"Do I just say, 'Jesus, I believe in You; take me in to Yourself...make me Your own. I do believe all these things I've read, but…do You really hear me? Is this all there is to it? Am I really talking to You, the Son of God?'"

Yes, my friend! *Yes*!

While you hesitate, let me tell you what God says in His own Word, in Proverbs 18:10 (emphasis added): "The name of the Lord is a strong fortress; **the godly run to Him *and are safe*"!**

Several years ago, a dear friend named Roger walked out of a recording studio I owned in West Hollywood after locking up at midnight. In a flash, a car pulled up to the curb, and three young thugs, high on drugs, grabbed him, threw him into the back seat of their vehicle, and drove off, yelling and cursing. In the back seat, one of the kidnappers was holding a sharp knife to Roger's throat—and it was obvious that the men were taking him somewhere to kill him.

Strangely calm, though afraid to move, Roger croaked, "Can I say something—?"

The guy with the knife answered menacingly, "Say what, you [unprintable words here]?"

The knife point already piercing his throat, Roger managed to voice these words: "Jesus loves you."

"Say *what*?" the guy replied, then he turned to speak to the driver, still speeding along: "*Stop the car*!"

Then, as he opened the door and grabbed Roger roughly, he told him, "*Get out*!"

They left him lying on the sidewalk and sped away into the night.

Roger lived to tell me this *because he could speak the name of Jesus.* The very name of the Lord was his protection, and he was saved that night from certain bloody death.

The Bible also says, "The salvation we preach is as near as your own mouth" (Romans 10:8), and, "Draw close to God, and God will draw close to you" (James 4:8).

Understand?

He does hear us; He hears you! Whenever the name of Jesus (Jeshua) is uttered, even in a whisper, He hears from heaven. His name is called—and **He is present.**

When His name is spoken derisively, in cursing and sacrilege, He hears that, too, as it happens way too often today. But that makes Him even more eager to respond to even a whisper spoken to Him in reverence…or worship…or praise…or in personal invitation to Him to save and claim a human soul.

Like yours.

The writer in Romans goes on to say, "**IF** you confess with your mouth the Lord Jesus and **believe in your heart** that God has raised Him from the dead, **you will be saved.** For with the heart one believes unto righteousness, and with the mouth confession is made **unto salvation**" (Romans 10:9, emphasis added).

I urge you: DO THIS NOW!

Don't wait another minute—HIS Holy Spirit is calling you, inviting you into His kingdom. Embrace Him, praise HIS Holy Name, Jesus. Make the vow in front of the watching and listening angels that you'll be devoted and faithful to Him as long as you live, coming and growing to really KNOW HIM…as He now KNOWS YOU!

As you do this, *a conception will take place in you.* You may or may not feel it immediately, but don't be alarmed if you don't. When you were conceived in your mother's womb, you didn't feel a thing. She may not have known of your conception either—but soon she did. Your new life made its presence felt.

I promise you that **IF** you did what I just asked, from your heart and mind, with real intention and new awareness, the NEW YOU will make its presence known to you and to others around you. You'll increasingly feel fresh, clean, and joyous. Perhaps to your surprise, you'll want to keep learning more and more of God's Word and His promises to you, as His child and blood-bought member of His forever family.

This is what's called being "born again." It means a new life is emerging and growing in you as you discard much of the "old you," like a cicada shedding its useless, old shell. Like a new infant, you will hunger and thirst for righteousness as a babe does for the mother's milk.

You'll want to know more and more about your Father and HIS Son, and how and why He loves you so much. Please get a New Living Bible translation, so you'll more easily understand what it says in modern English. Ask the Lord to guide you into a church fellowship, one that deeply respects and teaches God's revealed will—not liberal people's "revisions" and "new interpretations." *Look for a church that looks at God's words on the pages, believing exactly what they said two and three thousand years ago.* Those words have never changed, because God doesn't change—and you'll come to appreciate that fact more and more as you grow on your spiritual journey.

Baptism: Vital Outer Sign of Inner Change

Finally, for God's sake and your own, get baptized, calling on the precious name of the Lord Jesus. As the Bible makes so plain, baptism is a watery symbol of the burial of your own life and the resurrection to your new life. Immersion-in-water baptism is truly the same as the water burial and resurrection Jesus Himself deemed necessary for "fulfilling all righteousness."

DO IT! You'll thank the Lord Himself for the rest of your days for the NEW YOU, remembering the day and hour when you were buried to your old meandering life—and raised to a new, ETERNAL one!

I'm tearfully rejoicing with you, dear friend. We'll talk a

lot about this moment in heaven when we're together. What a day of rejoicing that will be!

Let me leave you for a moment with one last story, one I hope you'll identify with.

Many times, I've told about some of the three hundred or more baptisms that have taken place in our swimming pool at our home here in Beverly Hills. These have taken place because many churches don't baptize any more, scripturally or literally.

Several years ago, a friend called to tell me about her friend, Mary. Mary was a sweet, lovely eighty-year old who read about the baptisms in our pool and tearfully told our mutual friend, "You know—I was never baptized. I've considered myself a Christian for fifty years, but our church doesn't baptize like Pat Boone does in his pool."

Mary continued, "I'm old now, and *I don't know* [IF] *I'm truly saved.* I've hoped I was good enough, I've tried to please God all these years, but *I'm just not sure.* You say you know Pat Boone; do you suppose he'd be willing to baptize me?"

My friend called me with this message and soon she brought Mary to see Shirley and me at our home. What a sweet lady with her white hair, rosy cheeks, and innocent smile! We chatted a few minutes in our den, and soon I asked her, "Isn't it wonderful to know you belong to Jesus?"

Tears welled up in her eyes. "That's why I'm here," she

said. "*I don't know...*I hope I'm saved, but I don't feel it, I'm not sure. And that scares me."

I took her hand and asked, "Will you believe it, **IF** Jesus says you're saved?"

She nodded yes, but with questioning eyes, still teary. I opened my Bible and read Mark 16:16 to her:

> He who believes and is baptized shall be saved...; but he who does not believe will be condemned.

"Mary," I said, "these are Jesus' last words before He ascended to heaven after He rose from the dead. You believe in Jesus, don't you, as your Lord and your Savior?"

Quietly, she answered, "Yes, I do."

"So you believe. What else does He say?"

She answered, "Be baptized."

Then I said, "You're about to be baptized, Mary...*and you shall be saved*!"

We all got up—Mary, her friend, Shirley, and I. After a stop by the changing room, we went into the pool, with its water about chest high for Mary.

Raising my hand toward heaven, I said, "I baptize you, Mary, in the name of the Father, Son, and Holy Spirit." I lowered her backward into the water, completely immersing her, "burying her," and quickly raising her.

I'll never forget the surprised look on her drenched but joyful face! She was radiant, childlike, and laughing with delight.

Within moments, she had toweled off, slipped again into the changing room to get back into dry clothes, put away the bathing cap, uncovering her white hair, and come back into the house. We chatted a little, shared a brief, sweet prayer, and stood at the front door to say goodbye.

Mary's eyes again filled with tears, and I asked her why. Obviously trying to keep from crying, she exclaimed, "It's true! I know! I know!"

Then Mary and my friend left.

I learned later that she died one week after that day.

Mary had one week of "knowing" in her eighty years of living before she met face to face with the One who knows her even as she knows Him.

You want that, too, don't you, friend? I believe that **IF** you just do what we've shared these many hours, and **IF** you truly believe and totally trust in Jesus and His revealed Word... you will.

YOU WILL.

Part IV

A Living Faith

chapter eleven

Faith vs. Belief

After all this time and effort and communing together, I choose to believe you've got the message; you now (**IF** you didn't already) believe in God, in His divinely inspired Word, and in Jesus, His Son.

I hope and pray you've communicated directly with Jesus, acknowledged and accepted Him as your Savior, confessed the sinfulness in your nature, and asked for His eternal forgiveness. I also pray you're committing to find a Bible-believing church or fellowship that will baptize you into Jesus, as the Bible instructs.

That's an odd phrase, isn't it—"into" Jesus?

Yes!

Paul, a devout Jew who became the thirteenth apostle, explains:

> Have you forgotten that when we were joined with Christ Jesus in baptism, **we joined Him in His death**? For we died and were buried with Christ by baptism. And just as Christ was raised from the dead by the glorious power of the Father, now we also may live new lives.
>
> Since we have been united with Him in His death, *we will also be raised to life as He was!* (Romans 6:1–5, NLT; emphasis added)

My friend, that's what we call "*the gospel*"—the good news!

When this happens, you have put your whole past life—at least the sad, selfish, and sinful parts—totally behind you, as far as God is concerned. In fact, the Bible promises that "He remembers [our sins] no more" (Jeremiah 31:34). Isn't that great? You are a new person; you're as clean as a newborn baby. You're starting from scratch…again!

So, now what?

It's important to understand the difference between "faith" and "belief."

You *believe* my first three points, right? God exists, the Bible is His inspired Word, and Jesus is the Son of God.

Well, guess what?

So do Satan and all the demons in hell! They believe each of those truths, too.

James, the brother of Jesus and leader of the early disciples, declared:

> You say you have faith, for you believe there is one God. Good for you! Even the demons believe this and they tremble in terror. How foolish! Can't you see that faith without good works is foolish? (James 2:19, 20)

Don't get spooked! This isn't going to lead you into trying to "earn your salvation" by tirelessly following all kinds of rules and obligations and doing endless good deeds to prove your faith. That was the old way, the Mosaic way.

But when you properly understand the difference between faith and belief, it will all make perfect sense, and you'll be eager to demonstrate your new faith. Jesus Himself will work with you to do *what you truly want to do*. Good deal?

Explantation: That's not a typo. I want to "explain" and "plant" this in your mind. When you can see something with your own eyes and experience it with your natural senses, and when it's proven beyond doubt to your mind… you *believe.* That's what the demons do—because they *know* Jesus is real, and that His Father has prepared an eternal hell for them, which they know they can't avoid.

You now believe…because we've given you solid proof you can believe in.

But "faith"? God defines that word in Hebrews 11:1 "Now faith is the substance of things hoped for, *the evidence of things not seen.*" A belief, a hope so strong it's *virtually a substance*, becoming real as it is lived, prompted by and lived in *the evidence God provides daily.*

Get the difference? Seeing is believing, while *faith* is devoutly hoping for things you can almost taste and feel, they seem so real already, and it's trusting in the evidence that feeds that hope!

It's quite simply a new—and exciting—way to live, trusting in God to lead the way!

And He will!

That's what these final chapters are about: Faith. One of the most important "faith foods" is reading God's Word, which declares that "faith cometh by hearing, and hearing by the word of God" (Romans 10:17).

Well-Fed Faith

You and I both need to feed on God's Word every day, as I now do, to get nourished and build our absolute faith on the solid truth of what God has revealed.

IF we really want to know God, to know Jesus as He knows us, we have to feed on His Word. When Shirley and

I were in our early marriage and I had to travel so much, we doted on each other's letters, reading every word and wishing we could be together. I didn't know until years later that she was *saving every one of my letters and notes and cards*! I wish I could say the same, but in my busy packing and unpacking and traveling life, I've only recently found several wonderful, intimate love letters that she wrote me, and that I just couldn't throw away.

The latest discovery is one she had saved and sent our youngest daughter, Laury. In it, an eighteen-year-old college freshman named Pat, missing his nursing-school sweetheart, Shirley, wrote, confessing, "I think I love you. If I really know what love is, I think I really love you." That note meant so much to Shirley that she kept it for sixty-six years.

When I read it a few weeks ago, in my own handwriting, remembering the lovesickness I was feeling then and missing her so terribly now after sixty-five years of marriage, I cried and cried.

The whole Bible, especially the New Testament—which is focused on Jesus and how the Father provided "Salvation" (Jesus) to the world—is a massive love letter.

It is the greatest love letter ever written!

Faith in the Bridegroom

Remember John 3:16, which we've already looked at a couple of times? "For God so loved the world that He gave His only begotten Son"...who came as a defenseless little baby, grew up in obscurity, and lived a perfect, sinless life, then willingly gave His own life in a senseless, torturous crucifixion to prove how indescribably much He loves us!

Are you seeing this?

Jesus wants to marry us, you and me!

John the Baptist, when he first began to preach as God directed him, described the Messiah as the Bridegroom coming for His Bride (John 3:29).

Orthodox, traditional Jews understand this image. For at least three thousand years, the prescribed process was: man loves woman, becomes "engaged' or "betrothed" to her, then goes away, back to his own home and father, plans and prepares a home for the new twosome without telling her when he'll be back, then SURPRISE! With no warning, sometimes in the middle of the night, he comes back to claim his bride, telling her he's prepared a home for them. He stays for the wedding ceremony and then takes her away with him to their new home.

And "everybody lives happily ever after."

YES! That's what this is for you and Jesus.

Don't be hung up on "gender"—being male or female has nothing to do with this.

Jesus, the Son of God, agreed with His Father before

time began that He would come into the human condition, among men and women created in their very image. They agreed that He would live as a human, tell them who He was and why He'd come, and that He was searching for those who really would like to be part of God's forever family, and who would commit—be "betrothed"—to Him. Then they agreed that He'd go away to prepare an eternal Home for Him and His Bride.

That's the whole deal. He's absolutely done His part—all except for that big surprise: ***His Second Coming to take His completed and committed bride home with Him forever.***

Faith: It's a Simple Matter

I know this sounds strange, even bizarre, like a fairy fantasy to those who are totally ignorant of God and the massive true, historic account of His creation and involvement with mankind. It's all recorded in detail, and has been readily available to millions of us for thousands of years. But one of the strangest things about people (men often more so than women), is their curiosity *about* God—while resisting who HE Himself reveals He is! Many folks, especially those who are "enlightened," "intellectual," "world-wise," and "modern," feel these incontrovertible truths are too simple, childish, and "religiously restrictive" to accept.

But the supremely intellectual and scholarly Apostle Paul, in his letter to the Corinthian believers, wrote:

For the message of the cross is "foolishness" to those who are perishing, but to us who are being saved it is the POWER OF GOD. For it is written:

"I will destroy the wisdom of the wise, and bring to nothing the understanding of the prudent."…

For since, in the wisdom of God, since the world through its wisdom did not know God, it pleased God through the "foolishness" of the message preached to save those who believe.

For Jews request a "sign," and Greeks seek after wisdom; but we preach Christ crucified—to the Jews a stumbling block and to the Greeks foolishness—but to those who are called, both Jews and Greeks, Christ the power of God and the wisdom of God.

God has chosen foolish things of the world to put to shame the wise, and God has chosen the weak things of the world to put to shame the things which are mighty, and the base things of the world and the things which are despised God has chosen, and the things which are not—to bring to nothing the things that are,

That no flesh should glory in His presence. But *of Him you are* in Christ Jesus, Who became for us wisdom from God—and righteousness and sanctification and redemption—That, as it is written, "He who glories let him glory in the Lord." (1 Corinthians 1:18–31, emphasis added)

Please get this: God is deliberately choosing "foolish" methods—to confound and give excuses to men who are looking for them—to reject God's will for them!

Why am I spending so much of our time and space here on this?

Because God knew two thousand years ago, *and I recognize now,* that, in time, foolish "theologians" and "sophisticated" thinkers would discount and disregard the simple, direct, and unchanging truth about faith we're discussing here. He knew pompous scholars would not want a direct, stark, simple answer to the fundamental question, "What must I do to be saved?"

But He determined to keep it simple, stark, and direct!

When the much-respected Jewish leader Nicodemus came to Jesus secretly that night to "feel Him out" in person, the man started the conversation with Jesus like this: "Rabbi, we know that you are a teacher come from God; for no one can do these signs that You do unless God is with him" (John 3:2).

That was a nice, complimentary beginning to what Nicodemus hoped would be an involved, theological discussion. But Jesus didn't waste a second. He bluntly said to this honored Pharisee scholar, "**You must be born again.**"

"Say what?" a modern-day version of Nicodemus might say. "Did I hear you correctly, Jesus?"

Jesus' next statement was: "Most assuredly, I say to you, unless one is born of water and the Spirit, **he cannot enter the kingdom of God.**"

I can just see the respected intellectual, the highly educated leader, stunned, confused, unable to say anything except, "How is this possible?"

Assuming the man's question had been sincere, Jesus kindly answered with a brief lesson that included the powerful words:

> God did not send His Son into the world to condemn the world, but that the world through Him might be saved. He who believes in Him is not condemned—**but he who does not believe is condemned already,** because he has not believed in the Name [Jesus-Jeshua-Salvation] of the only begotten Son of God. (Emphasis added)

No complicated, convoluted answers. Just simple, direct, and to the point.

On the Day of Pentecost (see Acts 2), the Apostle Peter, who had denied that he even knew Jesus the night He had been arrested in the garden and sentenced to be crucified—after he had been emboldened by seeing the Risen Christ and having just been filled with the Holy Spirit—told the multiplied thousands confronting him and the other apostles that they had **crucified their own Messiah, the Son of**

God. Then he heard them cry out, as with one voice, "Men and brethren, what must we do?"

Peter didn't mince words or offer a course in biblical hermeneutics or apologetics. He simply answered at the top of his voice so everybody could hear:

> Repent, and let every one of you be baptized in the name of Jesus Christ [Jesus-Jeshua-Salvation] for the remission of sins, and you shall receive the gift of the Holy Spirit.

He added, of immense importance to you and me:

> For the promise is to you, and to your children, and to all who are afar off, and as many as the Lord our God will call.

That's us, friend—you and me.

Do you see the wisdom, the power, the persuasion of a simple, direct, unembellished answer? Not everybody will accept it—but no one can say they didn't hear or couldn't understand it!

In fact, Peter's blunt, simple answer was so persuasive that, right on the spot, on that very day:

> Those who gladly received his word were baptized; and that day about 3000 souls were added to them…

> saved…and they continued steadfastly in the Apostles' doctrine and fellowship, in the breaking of bread, and in prayers.

That was the birth, the conception, the formation of His Church (that word meaning "the called out" or the "called together"), His Bride, His flesh and blood and spiritual Body on this earth!

Faith is simple, stark, direct.

Like the word "IF."

Faith in Jesus is so simple, in fact, a child can understand it.

In Matthew 18, Jesus called a child to come to Him. He set the little one in the midst of this those gathered around Him that day, and said:

> Assuredly I say to you, unless you are converted and become as little children, you will by no means enter the Kingdom of Heaven. Therefore whoever humbles himself as this little child is the greatest in the Kingdom of Heaven.

You may be wondering why I'm stressing this simplicity, this directness, so much. I'm doing so because you've just begun your new life. In both biblical and literal terms, you're a "new creature"—a child again, but one who will grow quickly and triumphantly. Hallelujah!

Faith: Stands against Satan

I can guarantee you that, like Eve in the beginning of Creation, clean and fresh and belonging to her God, once you profess your faith in Him, you'll be targeted by the enemy of your soul and the enemy of your Savior. That enemy will present you with the same arguments and ask you the same questions he posed to Eve:

> Oh really? Did God say that? You fell for that? **IF** you just eat that inviting, delicious fruit that He planted there in the middle of the Garden Himself—you'll DIE? Oh, come on, that's ridiculous. Listen, you just got here, and I'm a lot more experienced around here. Let me tell you—that fruit tastes just as good as it looks, and it contains a potent brain-enhancer. Just a few bites of that fruit, and you'll be as smart as God. You'll know what's really "good" and what's evil or "bad." He'll try to convince you that things you want to do are evil, but they're not. And He'll try to get you to do things you don't want to do, saying they're "good," but really, they're not necessary. I'll set you straight: I can tell you're very naïve, and probably will just believe whatever God says, but I can advise you differently, and better. Go on, take a big bite, and you'll see.

This was Satan talking, and he was very persuasive, as usual. In his cunning, he appeals to our flesh, our desires.

Eve was naïve, childlike—and perfect. But God had given her and Adam the gift of their own will and reasoning power. He wanted them to love, respect, and obey Him, like His own kids. He wanted them to *choose Him,* not be programmed to only do His will, but to *want to do it.*

So He kept it simple. And he still does.

"Do this and live. Do that and die."

But Eve, and then Adam, chose not to have faith—in God and His plain words. Instead of choosing faith, they obeyed their own desire to taste the fruit and agreed with Satan that God didn't really mean what He said—and that they wouldn't really die.

Now you and I are condemned to die because *they* didn't have faith in what God said.

Since we all die because of that lack of faith, God decided that we could only *regain our eternal lives* by *reclaiming faith* in Him and His Word and by obeying Him—instead of disobeying and disbelieving.

To me, the symmetry, the perfection of God's Word and His plan for our redemption, is breathtaking. It makes perfect sense, it's righteous, it's just, it's fair.

Then Paul sums it up with finality:

> *Without faith it is impossible to please Him,* for he who comes to God must believe that He is, and that He is a

> rewarder of those who diligently seek Him! (Hebrews 11:6, emphasis added)

He demands that we **have faith in, obey, and "diligently seek" Him.** He will not give eternal life to those who pick and choose which of His commands to obey, and which to disregard as unnecessary, outdated, or too restrictive for today. No, those liberal theorists who arrogantly lead millions astray will find ample space with the demons in hell, those who "believe," but have no faith.

chapter twelve

Forgiveness: Faith in Action

As you know, the subject of these final few chapters is FAITH.

But what does that mean? Faith in *what*? Faith in the countless well-meaning but odious rules, traditions, new liberal inferences, and complicated excuses for abandoning God's direct orders and commands? Faith in who?

Oh, my friend—you can only put your faith in God's Word, and you really should read and feed on it yourself. I read the original Greek in college, but as I've said before, I love the New Living Translation or the New King James Version myself, because those translations offer language that I can readily understand without anybody's interpretation or explanations.

As a young Christian in Nashville, I read for myself in

Malachi 3 that tithes (one-tenth of a person's resources) and offerings were expected of me, and that God would "open the windows of heaven" to bless me if I was *faithful* in giving to Him…even if it was just from my small allowance. I've tried to be faithful in doing that ever since. I've never had a doubt about His provision for me since I read and put those simple words into action.

See what I'm saying?

Put your faith in God's Word, which says, "Let God's Word be true, and every man [who denies it is] A LIAR" (Romans 3:3, 4, emphasis added).

One important thing that Jesus expects—and directs—us to do is demonstrate our genuine *faith* as we obey and put into practice His "faith deeds." One of those faith deeds, which is absolutely essential—and is also a source of great joy and freedom—is *forgiveness.*

Offering forgiveness, a source of great joy and freedom, is not hard for some, but it's terribly difficult for others. Let's look again at part of the Lord's Prayer in Matthew 6:14, 15: "Forgive us our sins, as we have forgiven those who sin against us. And deliver us from evil."

But wait! Jesus adds a somber extension:

> **IF** you forgive those who sin against you, your heavenly Father will forgive you. But **IF** you refuse to forgive others, your Father will not forgive your sins.

See how simple, how direct—and how extremely serious! Jesus wants us to be like Him. He took upon Himself the sins of the whole world—many directed right at Him and His Father. He even looked down from the cross at the very ones who put Him there. And from that cross, in His dying voice, He said, "Father, ***forgive*** them…they don't know what they're doing! (Luke 23:34, emphasis added).

As always, Jesus lived out what He taught, setting a personal example of forgiveness for us. When one of His disciples had asked Him, "Lord, how many times must I forgive someone who sins against me—seven times?"

Jesus answered "seventy times seven."

In Matthew 18, Jesus tells the story of a man who was forgiven an unpayable debt by the king. Yet that man turned around and had another man imprisoned for owing him a relatively tiny debt. The king (representing Jesus, of course) was very angry. He had the original debtor—the man whose debt he had forgiven—thrown into a prison *from which he could never be released.*

Jesus summed it up like this:

> *So my heavenly Father will do to you…*[IF] each of you, from his heart, does not forgive his brother his trespasses.

Are you understanding why I am writing this?

God did not, through Moses, issue the "Ten Suggestions." No—His instructions are properly, and unmistakably, COMMANDMENTS.

I want everybody to realize that God's Son is just as emphatic. As God spoke through Moses, He was speaking through Jesus—and *He didn't give Adam and Eve a second chance.* If we shrug off and disregard Jesus, He won't be giving us a second chance, either. I truly wish I didn't have to say this—but it's *got to be said by somebody, and now*!

So, let's vow to truthfully and totally forgive, by acts of our own will, any and all trespasses and trespassers we feel have done us wrong. I can hear many protest, and say, "Easy for you to say, Pat...but you don't know what he/she did to me! I may try to forgive, but I can never forget—NEVER!"

I can identify and empathize with that. I've been attacked, undercut, deceived, ridiculed, and even robbed by people—even by those whom I trusted...and liked.

I know the human brain probably won't let us *forget* injustices and betrayals—but we *can forgive* by an act (repeatedly) of our will, saying it out loud, perhaps in prayer for God to help us, and even to forgive that person—as Jesus did from the cross, asking His Father to forgive the ones who were crucifying Him, asserting that they didn't know what they were doing.

Friend, nobody said it's easy to be a follower of Jesus. He

said Himself that we'd each need to "take up a cross" and do many things perhaps that aren't "natural," as He showed us Himself. But when we take Him at His word, and make genuine efforts, asking for His personal help—it's amazing what we *can* do.

The Bible, our wonderful guide, says, "For the joy that was set before Him, He endured the cross." Peter, *whom Jesus forgave for denying Him three times* (!), said:

> **You love Him even though you have never seen Him.** Though you do not see Him now, you trust Him; and you rejoice with a glorious inexpressible joy. **The reward for trusting Him will be the salvation of your souls.** (1 Peter 1:8, 9, emphasis added)

The point: There is great JOY—here and now—in forgiving. Forgiveness—just letting go and forgiving, from the heart—provides liberation from anger and resentment, freedom from having to keep score, and relief from constantly looking for retribution and revenge.

That's why Jesus commands it. He promises that we "will know the truth. And the truth will make [us] FREE!" (John 8:32, emphasis added).

Of course, there's so much more, so many habits and ingrained misconceptions to deal with. There are so many ways we can please our God and our Savior, Jesus, but those ways don't always come "naturally" to us. The idea of "working out our own salvation" personally is daunting, and hardly anybody seems eager to take on that challenge.

So let's not.

For now, in the newness of our acceptance of Jesus as our Heavenly Bridegroom, let's not dwell on the various important "must do's" that will prove our devotion to Him in our new and wonderful relationship with God, our Father. Hardly any of us can "do it all right, all the time," anyway. The Father knows that.

Let's take advantage of Jesus' own promise that *He'll do it all—through us*—IF we'll let Him.

Interested? Read on.

chapter thirteen

The Holy Spirit: Next-Level Faith

Your laws are wonderful.
No wonder I obey them!
The teaching of your word gives light,
So even the simple can understand.
I pant with expectation,
Longing for your commands.
Guide my steps by your word,
So I will not be overcome by evil.
O Lord, you are righteous,
And your regulations are fair.
Your laws are perfect
And completely trustworthy.
As pressure and stress bear down on me,
I find joy in your commands.

~Psalm 119:129–43

These words are found in the longest love song to God in the Bible, expressed by "a man after God's own heart," King David.

David was a rough man and a mighty warrior (he killed Goliath with one shot, remember?). He was also a sensitive man, a poet—as well as an adulterer and murderer.

A "man after God's own heart"?

Yes.

God has no perfect people to work with. But He tells us that He "looks on the heart." Even in the worst of us, He can identify *a heart that is willing to know Him,* to come to Him for rescue from our own failings, and to grow to love Him as His own.

That's what happened with King David after Nathan, the prophet, confronted him about one of the king's most grievous sins. David fell on his face and begged God for forgiveness, asking Him **not to take His Holy Spirit from him.** God heard David and forgave him (read the account of David's affair with Bathsheba in 2 Samuel 11, 12). Though David suffered consequences for his actions, he remained the king, made Israel a great nation, and fathered an heir to Israel's throne—the wise King Solomon.

Some time ago, I wrote and recorded a song, "The Fallen Giant," defending giants of history who made serious, usually career-ending mistakes, but who came back, through

God's grace, into prominence and made laudable contributions with their lives.

Adam and Eve were the first "giants"; they only made one grievous mistake we know of—*but that one mistake doomed the whole human race*! Yet God didn't forsake or destroy them; He made them father and mother of the human race He still believed would become His forever family.

Talk about "faith." God has always had more faith in us than we've ever had in Him. And after these thousands of years, *He's still believing in us*—at least those of us who will have and develop real faith in Him!

But "Pat," you say, "I'm still just human. I don't always do or say the right things. I'm not good at self-discipline, or even at knowing all the rules and regulations God expects me to follow. I sure don't think I can make myself do all you say He wants."

Got it. I hear you.

God hears you, too. That's one reason I believe He directed me to write all of this—for you.

He knows our weaknesses, our failings, our temptations. He became one of us, through His Son, Jesus, remember? And His Word says that Jesus "was tempted in all the ways we are—yet *without sin*" (Hebrews 5:14). Not one sin!

How did He do that? Is that possible?

Yes, it is possible…and He tells us how.

From the time I received Christ as a young teen until I had been married for ten years and had four daughters racing into their teens, I really tried to "work out my own salvation" with "fear and trembling," as God ordered through Paul in Philippians 2:12. I took that Scripture seriously, and as a husband, father, entertainer, and Christian, I made conscious efforts to do "all the right things" and not to think, desire, or do the many "wrong" things available—especially those that were accessible to a "pop star." You can imagine some of those things, I'm sure.

But I blundered, made mistakes, and put other things ahead of my main responsibilities. In a number of ways, I compromised my faith. Though I always tried to *look* righteous, I knew that, inwardly, I was messing up—in both big and little ways.

Finally, our marriage fell into trouble—because my very intuitive wife could tell I was changing, trying to really fit in with what's expected of a movie, recording, and television "star."

I knew that, inside my heart, I was a hypocrite.

But right when my life seemed like it was about to cave in, a magnificent Christian businessman (not a "minister") started telling me about the *Holy Spirit.*

if

Two Baptisms?

In my church background, there had been very little teaching on the Holy Spirit, the third Person of the Godhead—the Father, the Son, and the *Holy Spirit.* We believed that when we accepted Jesus and were baptized, that's all there was, and we were to read, learn, and obey everything God wanted us to do—*on our own*!

We felt we didn't need any miracles or supernatural abilities, as the first-century believers did; we had God's Word—we could read and understand and obey it—*on our own.*

I confessed this to my business friend, George Otis, when he brought up the subject of the Holy Spirit. He asked me *if I had ever asked Jesus to baptize me in the Holy Spirit.* Of course, I told him I hadn't—and nobody had ever told me that I should—or even what that meant.

He shook his head.

"No wonder you're having trouble being a good Christian!" he said. "You never read what John the Baptist said clearly about Jesus, God's Son, just before Jesus came to him to be baptized Himself? Look here!"

George turned to Matthew 3:11, where John told his followers:

> I baptize with water those who repent of their sins and turn to God. But someone is coming soon who

> is greater than I am—so much greater that I'm not worthy even to be His slave and carry His sandals! He will ***baptize you with the Holy Spirit*** and with fire! (Emphasis added)

Instantly, I saw there was a clear difference between water baptism and Holy Spirit baptism.

They're not the same thing.

Then I remembered that Luke, writing the first words of Acts 1:1, stated that Jesus appeared several times in the forty days after His resurrection, proving to hundreds that He was truly alive. He was actually eating with His apostles when He said, "Do not leave Jerusalem until the Father sends you the gift He promised; as I told you before, John baptized with water—*but in just a few days* you will be **baptized with the Holy Spirit**!" (Acts 1:5, emphasis added). He added, "*You will receive power* when the Holy Spirit comes upon you!"

Wasn't that what the angel Gabriel had said to the Virgin Mary?

> *The Holy Spirit will come upon you, and the Power of the Most High will overshadow you.* So the baby to be born will be Holy, and He will be called the Son of God. (Luke 1:35, emphasis added)

Clearly, the baptism of the Holy Spirit is different from the cleansing baptism of water!

But what does that difference mean? How does Jesus baptize us with (or in) His Holy Spirit?

God with Us

In just moments, George showed me. He took me to the passage about the Upper Room (see John 14), where Jesus was giving His last instructions and wisdom to His perplexed disciples. They couldn't believe He was telling them He was going to be crucified and taken from them. If that was true, how could they go on?

He told them:

> If you love me, obey my commandments. And I will ask the Father and he will give you another Advocate (Comforter, Instructor)—and He will never leave you! **He is the Holy Spirit, who leads into all truth.** The world cannot receive him, because it isn't looking for him and doesn't recognize him. But you know him, because he lives with you now and **later will be in you.** No, I will not abandon you as orphans—**I will come to you!**

He went on:

> All who love me will do what I say. My Father will love them, and we will come and **make our home with each of them.**

Are you getting this?

In the early moments of His agony, realizing his loving disciples (like you and me) were going to feel left behind, powerless and on their own, He was promising that God the Father and He the Son would come to our individual homes and LIVE WITH US!

How? By and in His Holy Spirit—the Third Person of God!

◈◈◈

We ought to stop here for a minute contemplate what we've just learned.

God came to earth in human form, and Jesus, the living Word (Jeshua, Salvation), became flesh and dwelt among us (John 1:14).

He walked, talked, healed, fed, and confronted the hypocritical religious leaders, went into people's homes, ate and drank with them, and loved them with an indescribable love. That was God the Son.

Then He, God in the flesh, promised He would come again in Spirit form and would come to our homes and live with us.

Vital question: Did Jesus promise salvation to everyone?

No. He wanted everyone to be saved, and voluntarily

gave His life for everyone—but remember, in His first public message, the Sermon on the Mount, He foretold that most would choose to take the broad way to hell. Only a relative few would enter the narrow gate to be saved. As I said earlier: *It is a choice each of us must make.*

It is the **IF** that will determine our destiny.

◈◈◈

As Jesus was saying goodbye to His disciples on the Mount of Olives just before He returned to heaven, He proclaimed:

> He that believeth and is baptized shall be saved. He that believeth not shall be condemned. (Mark 16:16)

How did we get saved?

WE ASKED!

We asked the "Saver"—the Savior—to save us! We ASKED Him to forgive us and cleanse us from our past sins. And He did!

How do we receive the Holy Spirit?

WE ASK!

It's not something that automatically happens when we're saved. God, in the person of the Holy Spirit, is polite, and He knows that not everyone who believes in Him and wants to be saved actually *wants to be filled with His Spirit, having Him direct, instruct, and be Lord over his or her personal life.*

I know I didn't.

When George Otis was explaining all this to me and I realized he was leading up to encouraging me to ask the Lord to fill me, baptize me, immerse me in His own Spirit, I was afraid.

I admit it.

On one hand, I wanted to know God's will for me and to receive truth, wisdom, and guidance from Him. On the other hand, what would He demand of me? Did I really want to make Jesus Lord of my life *now*, not just my Savior for eternity?

Then George asked if I was familiar with Revelation 3:20, where Jesus, proclaimed:

> Behold, I stand at the door and knock. **IF** anyone hears my voice and opens the door, I will come into him and dine with him, and he with me!

I told George I knew it well; I understood it as an invitation to any and all. But then my friend stunned me.

"Pat, He's talking to *the church* in Laodicea (Revelation 3:14), the one we call the 'lukewarm church,' where the believing members were well off, self-satisfied, and comfortable. He described them 'neither hot nor cold,' and wished they were one or the other, not just lukewarm. Of those who were lukewarm, He said, '*I will vomit you out of my mouth.*'"

Pretty blunt and emphatic, don't you think? This is the Lord talking to His own church members!

That's how strongly Jesus feels about "country-club Christianity," taking it easy because we have it easy, and not really looking to grow in faith and responsibility. And it's to nominal, "don't-get-in-too-deep," sometime believers that He says, "I'm knocking at the door of your heart. **IF** you'll invite me in, I'll *come into you, dine with you, go to work and play with you, change you inside out, and make you an overcomer in whatever you may ever face.*" Shouldn't we all want that, and welcome the everlasting, all-powerful presence of God Himself....*in us*?

George then reminded me that Jesus had clearly said:

> **IF** you, being evil, know how to give good gifts to your children, how much more will your heavenly Father give His Holy Spirit to those who ASK HIM! (Luke 11:13, emphasis added)

I had asked Jesus to *save* me, and He did. Now I knew I was to ask Him to *fill* me, *baptize me in His Spirit*...and I did.

And He did.

And I've never been the same.

On that same dramatic evening, George reminded me that, as Jesus was about to ascend to heaven, His last words to future total believers were:

> And these signs will follow those who believe: In My Name they will cast out demons; they will speak with new tongues; they will take up serpents; and if they drink anything deadly, it will by no means hurt them; and they will lay hands on the sick and they will recover. (Mark 16:17, 18)

That is, Spirit-filled believers may sometimes move in the supernatural, just like the believers in Jesus did in the first century! Mark records that the Lord performed these supernatural signs through the disciples, confirming the Word they were now spreading to the world.

This was the pattern, the way the church, the coming-together of Jesus' followers, grew in power and holy love to reach most of the world in those ancient days, and it's supposed to be the recurring pattern today.

And sometimes, when you might not expect it, supernatural—even miraculous—things can happen in the lives of "normal" people when the Holy Spirit knows He's needed.

Well along in my career, it had been well established that my family and I are Christians, through and through. So other Christians have always felt they can approach me with personal requests— which they absolutely can.

Once, a person I hardly knew got me on the phone and told me about her dear friend who was dying of cancer at St. John's hospital and asked if I'd go pray for her. How could I say no? I asked her for the friend's name, and she told me it was Rhoda.

Shirley and I went to the hospital and were shown to Rhoda's bedside, in a room with two others—with curtains around each bed for privacy. The dear woman, in her sixties, was in a coma, but I'd been told that often coma patients can hear, even if they don't open their eyes or seem to respond.

So I introduced myself and Shirley, and I spoke to Rhoda as if she might hear and know we were there.

"Rhoda, your friend has asked us to come and pray for you, and here we are," I said. "I don't know what your relationship may be with God, but I want you to know that He knows you and loves you. And your name is in the Bible! In the book of Acts, Jesus' disciples were huddled in a room together hiding from authorities because their leader Peter had been arrested and jailed for preaching publicly about Jesus.

"But the Bible recounts that, at midnight, angels put the soldiers guarding Peter to sleep, opened the jail door, and led him out into the night—free!

"He went to a place where he knew the other disciples were hiding and tapped on the door. A young woman

was asked to go look through the door opening to see who was there. The woman's name was Rhoda!

"She opened the door and let Peter in. He rushed to his brothers, and they all praised the Lord together!"

Then I went on:

"Rhoda, isn't it amazing that your name is in the Bible? And that same Bible says that Jesus stands at the door of our hearts, knocking. IF we'll open the door, He'll come in and live with us, in our hearts, and take us to heaven with Him when we die. I know He's knocking at your door now, Rhoda. Would you like Him to come in?"

As Shirley and I watched, Rhoda's expression didn't change, but we saw tears roll down her cheeks. We sensed that she was admitting her Savior into her heart.

One day, I'll meet Rhoda in heaven, I'm sure of it.

Gifts of the Spirit

God Himself is Spirit. Jesus is His physical manifestation, and the Holy Spirit is God Himself in invisible but all-powerful form, able to act in and through humans like us—IF *we're willing for Him to.*

The big question—the huge **IF** for us—is are we willing, and receptive of His Spirit?

The Apostle Paul, in 1 Corinthians 12, talks specifically

about the supernatural gifts and leadership offices that the Holy Spirit would distribute among believers: apostles, prophets, teachers, workers of miracles, healers, helpers, leaders, and those who can speak in tongues (or unknown languages). All of these gifts are supernatural, bestowed by God's Spirit into ordinary people who simply believe that God does what He says He will do.

But it's unfamiliar to us today, I know. Most churches don't really want to get into the realm of the supernatural, the "charismatic" (Holy Spirit gifting), precisely because they can't control it. Nobody knows for sure where the Holy Spirit may lead. In fact, Jesus told Nicodemus that the Spirit is like the "wind"; nobody knows where it came from or where it's going. That's unsettling to church leadership. So they want to keep everything natural (as opposed to "supernatural"), predictable, and polite—and they want to keep it inside the boundaries of no more than an hour a week.

But that's not Jesus' style!

He wants to rock our world; shake up the natural, human order; and wake us from lethargy and half measures of those who are playing it safe, not offending anyone or making anybody uncomfortable.

He wants to change us, fundamentally, from the inside out.

He wants to make us into NEW PEOPLE!

So how did He, knowing our natural reluctance to commit to a different lifestyle, one in which we're expected to change our ways and live like the new creation we've become spiritually, help make it possible?

Read again the dire-sounding Philippians 2:12: "Work out your own salvation, with fear and trembling." Keep going into the next verse: "For it is *God who works in you* both to will and to do for His good pleasure"!

You see? He doesn't leave us on our own. **IF** we ask Him to live in us "by His Spirit," He will cause us to WANT to do His will—and then He will give us the POWER to DO IT!

Here's the question, the big "**IF**" here. Do you have to be baptized in the Holy Spirit to be saved?

No.

You can go along through the rest of your life trying to please the Lord, trying to be a good, church-going Christian, sometimes living as you know you should—and often not. You can wonder why some of your believing friends seem so happy all the time, even when they're going through severe trial and disappointment, even physical disability.

What is they have that you don't?

Most likely it's the Holy Spirit within them.

Just today, in my home church, a man stood in the service

and asked if he could tell us what the Lord had just showed him. He's in the car business and said Jesus conveyed this to him (paraphrasing):

> You buy a car, and you get a very good price you're happy to pay. Then come the add-ons, accessories, further options that make driving the car more enjoyable...and the price goes up, often considerably.
>
> But when you come to Jesus and willingly pay the price of surrendering your life to God, you not only get the salvation freely—but the "accessories," the further enablements, also come free! But you have to ask for them. They're "optional."
>
> But you're foolish to drive the car without them, when you don't have to. The Holy Spirit is literally Jesus coming into you, at your invitation, to guide and strengthen and help you be MORE than you can ever be on your own!

My dear friend, evangelist Kenneth Copeland, whom I first knew when we were much younger, was a rather wild child. After he surrendered his life to the Holy Spirit, he has said many times, "I still smoke and drink and cuss as much as I want to...*but Jesus changed my 'want to's*!"

The major, so important, point is this: **IF** you ask the Holy Spirit to baptize you in His Spirit and come and live in you, you'll see yourself becoming a new creature, a different person with different appetites, different desires, *a new* *hunger for God's Word,* and an unusual new love for people you haven't even liked. You'll also see many other happy changes. Friends will notice that something's happened to you; you will seem different to them somehow.

You'll find you're actually able to experience the admonition of 2 Peter 2:14,15:

> Live clean, innocent lives as children of God, shining like bright lights in a world full of wicked and perverse people. Hold firmly to the Word of Life.

Sounds good, doesn't it? But it's a tall order, **IF** we're trying to do it on our own. Because we're not supposed to. God wants to do it *through* us. In us. For us!

The Spirit Makes Us Ready!

Let me give you another example, right from Jesus' own lips, in the story about the five wise and five foolish virgins. In Matthew 25, as the time of betrayal and crucifixion were bearing down on Him, Jesus gave this dramatic scenario to emphasize the *necessity to be prepared for the coming of the Bridegroom for His bride, when it happens* (remember, you and I need to be included as His "Bride").

There were ten virgins—young, unmarried girls, part of the wedding party—anxiously awaiting the coming of the Bridegroom. Each had oil-burning lamps to light His entrance. But as the night was passing and the Bridegroom hadn't come yet, the oil in the lamps of the five foolish virgins ran out—and they were sleeping, too.

Suddenly, the cry rang out, "He's coming! He's almost here!"

The five wise virgins lit their lamps, and the foolish ones cried out, "We're out of oil! Please give us some of yours." The wise ones replied, "We only have enough for our own lamps! Go out and buy some more for yourselves!"

While the five foolish girls ran out to look hopelessly for more oil, the Bridegroom came...and the five foolish virgins were *locked out.*

In Jesus' own words, the negligent virgins came back, begging to come into the wedding, crying out, "Lord, Lord, open to us!" But He answered and said, "**I do not know you!**"

He (Jesus) concluded: "Watch therefore, for you know neither the day nor the hour in which the Son of Man is coming."

Please, dear friend, understand this. The *oil in the lamps* is the *Holy Spirit*! Oil, in the Bible, is always understood as the anointing of the Holy Spirit, poured on kings and prophets and chosen people, prescribed by the New Testament writer James as a "healing agent" when praying for the sick—the presence and power of the Lord's Spirit.

In this parable of the wise and foolish virgins, Jesus is clearly describing His Second Coming to judge the world and having to deny those, even those who were invited to be part of the wedding, because they were *trusting in themselves and their inadequate, insufficient preparation—and were not filled with His Spirit to make them ready*!

DON'T WAIT FOR THE LORD TO FILL YOU WITH HIS HOLY SPIRIT… ASK HIM TO DO IT NOW! OTHERWISE, YOU MAY WAIT UNTIL IT'S TOO LATE.

Remember, in John 8:31–32, Jesus said: "**IF** you abide in my Word, you are my disciples indeed. And you shall know the TRUTH, *and the truth shall make you free*"—"**IF**… **IF**… **IF** you abide in my Word, seek my face, show by your actions, your decisions, your priorities in your daily life, that your true desire is to be like Jesus." I know this isn't easy; we're human beings, not angels—and we need the very daily help of God's Holy Spirit to live out our good intentions, don't we?

I do.

We all do.

chapter fourteen

Special Invitation from Jesus

So now, I want to share with you something that's intensely personal. It's a revelation from God Himself, something that's been right in front of me—in front of all of us—for most of our lives. But, like many other things from God, it's so obvious that we overlook it; we miss it!

It's miraculous, it's divine, it's holy—and yet we can, and should, experience it every day. Like the appearance of the sun each morning, so hugely miraculous but so commonplace in our experience that we don't even bother to look at it, so the *appearance and presence of the SON of GOD in our own home can be overlooked* and taken for granted, as almost of no account!

What on earth am I talking about?

Prayer.

What is prayer?

Why…it's simply talking to God, isn't it?

We say things to Him, such when we say grace before meals, but He doesn't talk back. We don't hear anything in response; we just speak it and go on and eat. Right?

That's what we do and how we do it.

But **IF** prayer means anything at all, it presumes that *God is hearing us.*

And **IF** it means anything at all, it presumes that *God is in the room…with us*!

◈◈◈

Listen to me now, my dear friend, and this will change your life, forever.

Rather, listen to Jesus Himself, again in Revelation 3:20:

> Behold, I stand at the door and knock. **IF** anyone hears my voice and **opens the door,** I will **come in to him and dine with him, and he with me.**

Yes—we will dine with him, and he will dine with us!

JESUS WANTS TO HAVE DINNER WITH YOU!

◊◊◊

Can we…shouldn't we…pause for a minute?

I've read this verse many times. I've referred to it at least twice in this book. Yet—like almost everybody else, I've passed over it, considering it to be a figure of speech not to be taken *literally*, of course.

But I've just realized it, my dear reader, that—like *everything else Jesus ever said—He means it*!

Literally.

He wants to come by our side, wherever we'll let Him, and share lunch, or breakfast, with you…with me! Friend, I didn't fully realize or accept that till today! My Father woke me up this morning to make me understand He means **exactly what He says!**

I remember when the girls were little, we had family devotionals at breakfast before I rushed them to school each day. Shirley or I would read a short Bible story, we'd sing a "church song" together, have a brief prayer—and then off we'd go to school. That's the way we started our days. For more than ten years, *we had breakfast with Jesus*!

And what wonderful young women those little girls have grown up to be.

Coincidence?

My mind races back to instances in the Gospels where Jesus was openly condemned by "religious leaders" for eating and drinking in the homes of people who were notorious sinners. For example, there was Levi, a notorious tax collector, and his equally sinful friends. Jesus enjoyed their company and ate heartily enough that the religious leaders called Him (ridiculously) a "glutton and winebibber"!

On a different occasion, Jesus called another tax collector, the short-in-stature Zacchaeus, to come down from the tree he had climbed outside Jericho in an effort to see Jesus passing by. Jesus went to Zacchaeus' house *for dinner* and changed the man's life forever!

Jesus was also *having dinner* with Mary and Martha right after He called Lazarus from the grave where he'd been buried for four days!

It was during what we Christians call the Lord's Supper—the Jewish Passover, which is a *dinner commemoration*, Jesus broke bread and passed wine to His disciples, saying, "Take, eat, and drink—this is my body and blood that I'm sacrificing for you!"

Wait now—you and I must see this together.

This unprecedented incident is more than a dramatic scene. Far more than a religious ritual, it's a personal, intimate look at Jesus' emotional plea: "**As often as you do this, do it in remembrance of Me.**" Looking at the next few months and down through the ages, He was *asking you and* *me to frequently take of His body and His blood*, in the piece of bread and the cup of grape juice, visualizing and *"remembering" the moments when He did this very thing!*

God Himself, in the body of His Precious Son, is inviting Himself **into you**—in a divine meal for which He printed the invitation in His Word, recorded in the Upper Room in the midst of an actual meal with those He loved enough to die for—the very next day.

My friend, the Creator of all mankind literally waits eagerly for you to accept His invitation, whenever you're ready! He wants to be there when you eat and drink, remembering Him!

Please understand this dramatic truth—He became a human so He could know what we're like, and He enjoyed the experience! He loved our food, our drink, our sleep, our normal activities. And he wants us to know that He enjoys our company, even our human frailties and difficulties, and wants to help us with our human needs. He understands us! He enjoys our enjoyments (if they're good ones)!

And it was by the Sea of Galilee after the resurrection, the Risen Christ called to the disciples who had gone back to their fishing, believing He was dead. When they arrived, *they found Him at an open fire, cooking fish* for them to eat WITH HIM!

Also after the resurrection, Jesus joined two dejected disciples leaving Jerusalem on the road to Emmaus. Neither man recognized Him, and they invited the traveler to join them for dinner at the inn they had come to. *As Jesus "broke the bread" in front of them while they were eating together, they suddenly knew who He was!* As the excited pair is later telling their fellow disciples about how Jesus had appeared and eaten with them, Christ Himself suddenly appeared in the room with them! He asked, "Why are you frightened? Look at my hands and my feet; touch me—see that I'm not a ghost. Then, in their stunned speechlessness, disbelief, and awe, He casually asked, "Do you have anything here to eat?" Once they produced a piece of fish and some honey, *He ate it in their presence as they watched* (see Luke 24:35–42).

Why did He do this—and why is it recorded for us today? It's so we know for sure how much he loves us, and how much He wants to be intimately involved in our daily, natural lives. Yes, He's supernatural, but He's also natural. That's why He came from heaven and took on human form, so He…and we…could know He feels what we feel, hungers like we hunger, and enjoys what we enjoy.

I believe He wanted to make the disciples then and us today realize that He's always aware of our needs, and that He *wants to be involved* in even our mundane activities; *He enjoys being with us*!

I'll bet you have heard about the great wedding feast in heaven prepared for those who collectively have become Christ's Bride to celebrate their eternal salvation and virtual marriage to the Lamb of God (see Matthew 22). As we're told, some will be sitting to His right; others will be seated on His left...*eating, drinking,* and *communicating,* and *loving and rejoicing...together.*

These thoughts have hit me so hard, so wonderfully, so excitingly:

JESUS WANTS TO HAVE DINNER WITH YOU. HE KNOCKS AT YOUR DOOR—HE WANTS TO JOIN YOU AND ENJOY YOU WHILE YOU EAT!

If He didn't want to, He wouldn't have said it so dramatically and simply as among His last words in the Bible! This is His last invitation to those who profess belief in who He is, why He lived, and why He died for us.

◊◊◊

Eating is how we live, isn't it?

When we quit eating—we die.

Eating should be—and for most of us is—one of life's great joys.

Well, Jesus is life Himself, in the flesh...eternal Divinity incarnate.

Why would He *not* want to be welcomed into our personal, private pleasure and enjoy it with us? HE CREATED WHAT WE'RE EATING! And, like any great chef, He wants to delight in us enjoying His creation.

But much more than that, He wants to *have conversation with us—while we're eating,* **IF** *we're willing*!

I'm very serious. We talk to others while we're eating, don't we? Sometimes we feel kind of lonesome when we eat by ourselves. But, with Jesus our friend, *we never have to.* In fact, Jesus' own natural brother in James 4:8 declares emphatically: "Draw near to God and He will draw near to you." And the apostle Peter urges us, "Cast all [your] cares on Him, **for He cares for you**"!

My dear, dear reader friend, God loves you so much that He gave His life for you! Should you—or I, God help me—be *surprised* that He wants to come to you, knock on the door of your heart, and hear you invite Him in, just as when you say grace or ask His blessing on the food?

Well then, encourage Him to sit down while you eat and perhaps sometimes whisper precious words of advice, counsel, and encouragement to your mind, continually assuring you that *you're important to Him,* and that *He wants to help you succeed* in every worthwhile thing you want to do.

If you're lucky enough to have family and friends with you while you eat, talk about your Savior and what He's showing you in His Word. Encourage those around you to do the same, as if your Guest was right there with you… *BECAUSE HE IS!* That's exactly what Shirley and I used to do with our four daughters—and we even took Him in the car with us on the way to school!

I suggest, humbly, that you keep your Bible near you whenever you can, while you're eating, so when God gives you a thought, or when you have a concern or question, you can look it up. *Keep listening and learning, and He'll find ways to teach you what He wants you to know.* He's been doing that for me all these years now—and I'm still learning, and always will be, **IF** I keep my focus on Him and His Word.

◊◊◊

The WORD, the WORD, the WORD!

Again, the WORD, the WORD, THE WORD!

And that ominous word, "IF"!

My dear friend, I've come to know—and love—God's revealed WORD. There is no other source of wisdom—and truth—and life-saving love than God's Word!

But tragically, disastrously, too few people even know God's Word or have any desire to. So many influential people confidently proclaim we're "all basically good." "God loves us all," they say; "He'd never consign good people (like us) to a hell—which probably doesn't exist anyway!"

Oh, we're so good at deciding how we think things *ought* to be, how we'd like them to be, that we keep saying those made-up philosophies as if they were true, and we even convince others. They sound good, don't they?

My point?

I see us doing the same thing with our beloved country.

Just as America is in danger of losing its political and spiritual DNA through ignorance, apathy, and abandonment of the principles that made us great, we individually are in *terrible danger* of *losing our eternal lives* for the same reasons.

The only way we'll save America is to return and rededicate ourselves to what made us great in the first place. The early historian and political analyst Alexis de Tocqueville said famously, "America is great because America is good. If she ceases to be good, she will cease to be great."

In the same way, the Body of Christ, His Holy Bride, can only survive in the howling gales and subversive tides of liberal theology and abandonment of rock-solid, unchanging commandments of God by keeping our house built on the Rock, and not on shifting, sinking sand (see Matthew 7:24–25).

YOU AND I AREN'T GOD. Only He, and He alone, makes the rules and decides how things ARE…and will always BE.

I've counted them. **There are more than fifteen hundred "IFs" in the Bible.** With each one comes incredible blessing of God on one side and dire consequences on the other—including, in many instances, the loss of individual eternal life.

You may feel I've seemed harsh, strict, even personally

judgmental in parts of this book. But if you go back and check, I think you'll see that *I haven't been expressing my own opinions.* I wouldn't have done this to try to convince you of what *I* think.

No, like a fireman waking up a sleeping family to tell them their house is on fire and they have to hop up and get to safety, I've felt led—*no, compelled*—to sound a major alarm to help well-meaning people everywhere wake up, read God's Word for themselves, and do what He says to avoid the very fires of hell.

It's that serious.

As I'm winding up this *effort of love* on my part, my "cry in the wilderness," perhaps, wanting and personally needing to reach out to as many as may listen… with the Word of God (again, it's not my own thinking or ideas), knowing that I've only scratched the surface of all that our loving Father and His Savior Son want us to know and profit by eternally, *I beg you to open your own Bible and read it, cover to cover.*

God, by His Holy Spirit, will speak to you. Yes, TO YOU. He told His people long ago, through the majestic prophet Isaiah:

Seek the Lord while He may be found,
Call upon Him while He is near.
Let the wicked forsake his way
And the unrighteous man his thoughts;
Let him return to the Lord,

And He will have mercy on him,
And to our God,
For He will abundantly pardon.
"For My thoughts are not your thoughts,
Nor are your ways My ways," says the Lord.
"For as the heavens are higher than the earth,
So are My ways higher than your ways,
And My thoughts than your thoughts.
So shall my Word be that goes forth from my
   Mouth:
It shall not return to me void,
But it shall accomplish what I please,
And it shall prosper in the thing for which I sent it.
For you shall go out with joy
And be led out with peace."
   (Isaiah 55: 6–9, 11–12)

Okay, my friend...I'm through.

If, as I suppose, you've stayed with me this far, I'm hoping and believing that we are now brothers and sisters in the Lord, miraculously and eternally members together of God's forever family. If so, the Holy Spirit will keep us linked in prayer and communion with the Father and the Son.

We may not meet in person until, in what will seem like the winking of an eye, we'll embrace in that indescribable place Jesus said He has gone to prepare for us, "That where I am, there you [we] may be also" (John 14:2).

That's you and me—with Jesus and our **saved** loved ones!

Till then, I urge you to stay immersed in His Word daily, as every syllable becomes more precious each time you read it, including those like these from the "man after God's own heart," the psalmist David:

> You have done many good things for me, Lord,
> Just as you promised.
> I believe in your commands; now teach me good
>   judgment and knowledge.
> I used to wander off until you disciplined me;
> But now I closely follow your word.
> You are good and do only good; teach me your
>   decrees....
> You made me; you created me.
> Now give me the sense to follow your commands....
> Now let your unfailing love comfort me, just as you
>   promised your servant
> Surround me with your tender mercies so I may live,
> For your instructions are my delight.
>   (Psalm 119:65–68, 73, 76–77, NLT)

◈◈◈

My dear friend, my faithful reader, how can I adequately thank you for staying with me all this way? The best and most important way I can think of is to call your attention again to the even more imminent, drawing-closer **reality** of the *first words* at the *beginning of this effort of love and concern on my part.*

See you in heaven, brother or sister. And it won't be long, now.

Your brother, Pat

IF anyone serves Me, let him follow me;
And where I am, there my servant
will be also.

IF anyone serves Me,
Him my Father will honor.

~JOHN 12:26

And **IF** anyone hears My words and
does not believe, I do not judge him;

For I did not come to judge the world,
But to save the world.

He who rejects Me, and does not
receive my words,

Has that which judges him—
the word that I have spoken

Will judge him in the last day.

~JOHN 12:47, 8

Behold, I am coming quickly!

Blessed is he who keeps the prophecy
of this book.

He who is unjust, let him be unjust
still; he who is filthy let him be
filthy still; he who is righteous, let
him be righteous still; he who is
holy, let him be holy still.

For I testify to everyone who hears the
words of the prophecy of this book:

IF anyone adds to these things,
God will add to him the plagues
that are written in this book,

And **IF** anyone takes away from the
words of the book of this prophecy,

God will take away his part from the
book of life,
From the holy city—

And from the things which are
written in this book:
I am coming quickly

He who testifies to these things says,
"Surely I am coming quickly."

~Jesus, in Revelation 22

Appendix A

Snapshots and a Few Personal Stories

The Early Years

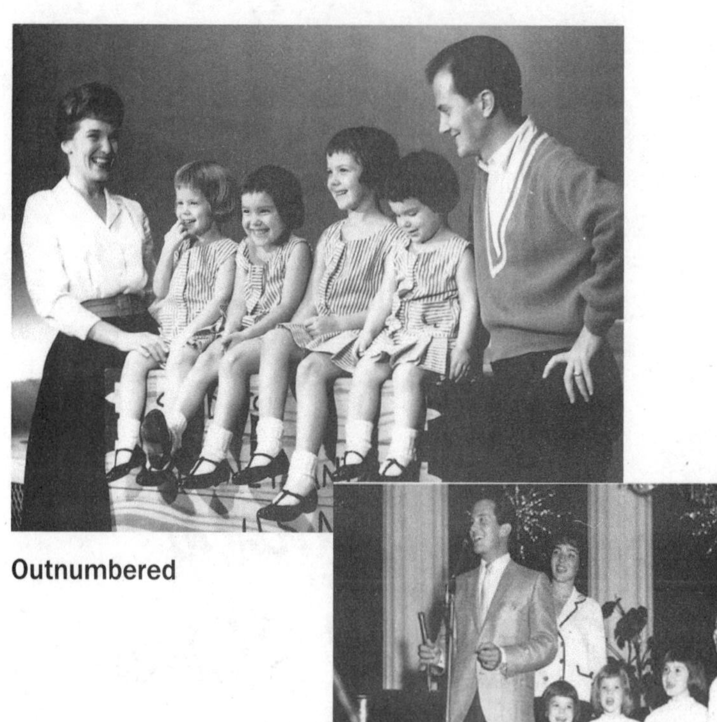

Outnumbered

The singing Boone kids—all of us!

Six people, one bike, a short trip in New Jersey

Shirl and me on graduation day, Columbia University, 1958

Loyal fans greeting the Boones when we moved to LA

Shirley, me, the Reagans, and the Easter Seals poster child

Parenting with a Future President

Shirley and I became good friends with Ron and Nancy Reagan when our kids went to the same school as their kids, Ron and Patti, in a wonderful school in the hills of Bel Air. Yes, Ron and Nancy were twenty-five years older us, but they had their kids toward the end of their childbearing days—while we had rushed ours while I was still in college.

When we attended all the grade-school functions, Ron and I would stand talking in front of a big fire in the fireplace of the main hall afterwards, talking politics. He was traveling then as a spokesman for GE, making what became known as "the speech"—the one in which he's famously quoted for saying, "Government is not the solution to our problems... *Government is the problem*!"

I was so impressed with his thinking and articulate way of expressing it, I remember saying to Shirley several times as we were driving home, "That Ron Reagan ought to run for office—he'd make a great congressman!"

Politically Incorrect?

I appeared on Bill Maher's aptly named *Politically Incorrect* television show several times; he liked me because he knew I would take the conservative side of issues...but with some humor.

The first time I was his guest, the discussion was about the Moral Majority, an organization founded by Jerry Falwell as a way for Christians to campaign for morality on TV and in our entertainment culture. Other guests included comedian Chris Rock, Frank Rich of the *New York Times*, and television commentator Paula Zahn. It was a very one-sided discussion, with the liberal guests inveighing against us "Bible thumpers" to try to force their views on everybody else. Bill, of course, a militant strident atheist, was loving it—but he kept looking sideways at me, because I wasn't saying anything.

Carefully choosing my spot to jump into the dialogue, I finally asked, "Do we all agree the Constitution is a good document?"

Everybody in the discussion agreed, saying that's what this was all about, anyway: freedom of speech.

I then asked, "Have you stopped to realize that document was written by a 'moral majority' guaranteeing everybody a right to express his or her religious views?"

Immediately, the guests began spouting out things like, "That's not the 'moral majority' we're talking about!"

"No," I answered. "That didn't exist then in today's form—but almost every signer of the Constitution was a churchgoing Christian—and you want to keep people who think like that silent today, not even to voice their opinions!"

The panel, even Bill himself, had no answer, so they switched the topic to prostitution, which every panelist except me, of course. all defended as a "necessary evil." As Chris expressed it, "Men need [prostitutes] 'cause they don't get it at home; the poor women need it to take care of themselves and maybe a kid; and it cuts down on rape and assault. Besides, what's wrong with it? Remember, it's the world's oldest profession!"

At that point, I interjected my comment: "Quit saying prostitution is the world's oldest profession—it is NOT!"

Chris said, confrontationally, "Oh yeah—what is?"

"Gardening," I answered.

There was stunned silence for a couple of seconds, while everybody started making the connection to the Garden of

Eden. Then the audience roared with laughter—and while Bill quickly took us to commercial, I heard Chris Rock muttering, "I set him up—I set *Pat Boone* up!"

With President Bill Clinton and others when he signed a resolution enacting National Parents' Day

With President George W. Bush, my friend

Appearance with Sean Hannity on TV

"Speedy" (me) meeting with Netanyahu May 13, 2018

With Bill O'Reilly

President Reagan, Charlton Heston, and me having dinner privately

With President Eisenhower

Some Faces You Might Recognize

With Andy Williams

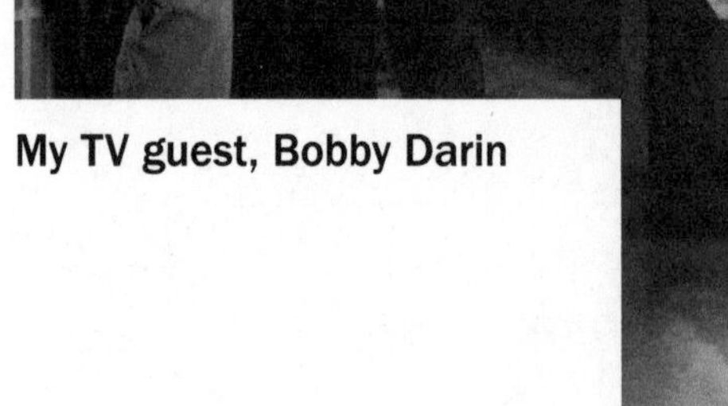

My TV guest, Bobby Darin

Anka, Avalon, Boone, Davis

Some Faces You Might Recognize

James Taylor and me backstage at his concert

My fan and friend, John Lennon

With Johnny Cash

I shocked the 'King of Shock Rock,' Alice Cooper, at the American Music Awards.

Some Faces You Might Recognize

Snoop Dogg and I on *The Test* TV show (he smelled funny)

With Dick Clark and Jerry Lee Lewis

With Charlton Heston in Israel

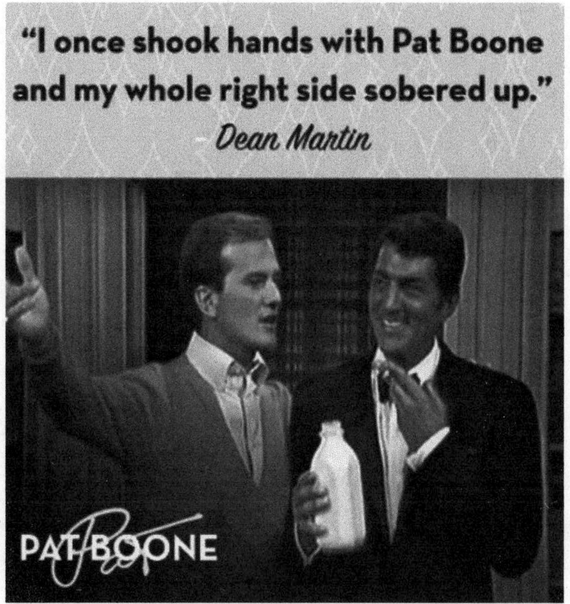

Joking around with Dean

Dean Martin and I were good friends, though we sure lived different life styles. Though he had a lovely wife, Jeannie, and several kids, he lived a pretty swinging life and seemed to enjoy the heck out of it. We played golf some together, and I appeared as a guest on his NBC TV show. He did drink, but perhaps not as much as he let on, because that was part of his persona. One night on his television program, Dean told Phil Harris, another famous drinker, "You know that Pat Boone fella? He's so religious—I shook hands with him the other day, *and my whole right side sobered up*!"

That got such a great laugh from the audience that I started repeating it in my own shows for years after that. I learned that people like it when you can kid yourself and take a joke. I've taken a lot of 'em.

Doing What I Love

Boones' TV humor

Live performance

My heavy metal phase

Presenting my "Exodus" lyrics at Yad Vashem, Israel

Doing What I Love

The man in white

A golfer with guts

Playing basketball in senior games at age eighty

Family, Friends, Faith, and Philanthropy

My favorite picture of two married lovers

Just one family group, baby daughter Laury's family

Silliness all around

Shirley, Billy Graham, and me—a loving bond

Mr. and Mrs. In Love out on the town

With grandson Ryan at Ryan's Reach

fundraiser

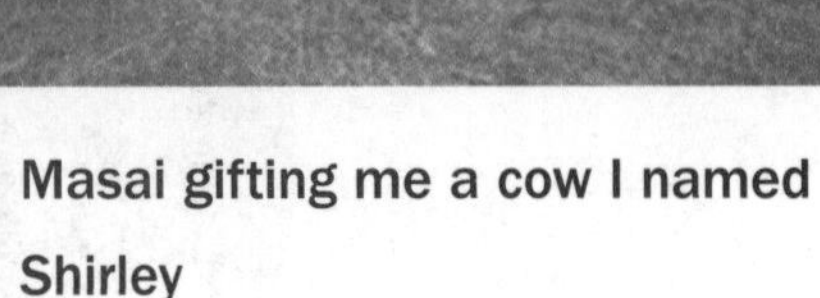

Masai gifting me a cow I named Shirley

Eighty-foot freshwater well drilled in Tanzania

Appendix B

Relics and Revelations

I wish I could hand you right now a copy of my aforementioned book, *Questions about God...and Answers That Could Change Your Life,*[14] which deals in much greater detail with the three questions I asked (about the existence and truth of God, the Bible, and Jesus) when I was honestly searching for the basis for my own faith, wondering if I was just the product of religious ideas, theology, and practices handed down to me by my parents.

You and I aren't together right now, so I can't do that. But, because the main object, the purpose, of this book is based so solidly and incontrovertibly on the evidence I gathered for that one, I need to offer a few more details to those who would like to dig a little deeper. (Much of the following information in this appendix about the first two questions

I asked in my own faith journey is drawn directly from that book.)

How Do We Know There's a God?

Couldn't Have Just "Happened"!

Among the countless reasons to sanely reject any idea of a godless cosmos, consider that things aren't always what they seem. As you read this, you probably think you're sitting perfectly still. But nothing could be farther from the truth. Right now, you're moving at four incredible speeds simultaneously:

- First, you're spinning in an easterly direction at 1,044 miles per hour. That's the speed at which the earth turns on its axis.
- Second, you're moving through space at 67,000 miles per hour—the speed at which earth orbits the sun.
- Third, you're orbiting the Milky Way's galactic center at 490,000 miles per hour. That's the speed at which everything in the galaxy spins around the Milky Way's center of mass.
- And fourth, as the universe expands, everything in it is hurtling outward at lightning speed (the speed varies depending on the object's location).

Yet even that's not the end of the story: The *expansion rate itself is accelerating*!

Now, look more closely at this book and at every other inanimate object around you. Everything you see (as well as you yourself) is a seething mass of microscopic and submicroscopic whirling activity, forces of light, mass, and energy in constant motion, with incredible power. Research into nuclear fission and fusion has proven that there is enough stored and active energy in a rock the size of a basketball to provide *all the energy needs for a city the size of Cleveland for a month*!

My point?

Is it not caveman-type idiocy to accept for one moment that all that we see and know, and all that we ourselves *are*, just "happened" or "evolved"?

Yet that's exactly what's being taught in our top schools and institutions of "higher learning" today, precisely because many experts and professors don't want to and will not accept the simple and obvious fact that God created all there is.

And that God Himself….*IS*!

Human Brain: Hard-Wired for God?[15]

Interestingly enough, scientific evidence shows that the human brain may, in fact, be hard-wired to believe in God. A report in the *Los Angeles Times* details research by neuroscientist Andrew Newberg, a professor at the University of Pennsylvania, whose findings show that humans in a meditative state experience a "higher reality," an intense state of awareness he has documented in brain scans. Newberg's model is based on research begun in the 1970s by psychiatrist and anthropologist Eugene d'Aquili.

"D'Aquili's theory described how brain function could produce a range of religious experience, from the profound epiphanies of saints to the quiet sense of holiness felt by a believer during prayer," writer Vince Rause wrote in the *Times*.

D'Aquili and Newberg had teamed up in the early 1990s, refining and testing the theory. Using imaging technology, they mapped the brains of people of faith, including Franciscan nuns "engaged in deep contemplative prayer," Rause said. "The scans photographed blood flow—indicating levels of neural activity—in each subject's brain at the moment that person had reached an intense spiritual peak."

The scans showed that, at peak moments of meditation and prayer, "the [neural] flow was dramatically reduced," Rause reported. "As the orientation area was deprived of information needed to draw the line between the self and the world—the scientists believed—the subject would experience a sense of limitless awareness."

Rause—who coauthored a book with Newberg called

Why God Won't Go Away—said his partnership with the neuroscientist began after Rause had been wracked by a series of personal tragedies. Rause lost his mother to cancer and his father to heart disease; he also lost four uncles, an aunt, and a grandmother.

"The cumulative effect of all the grief sent me reeling," he wrote. "I tried to find solace in prayer, but the words felt all wrong in my mouth." He tried to rekindle the faith of his childhood, but many years had passed. It seemed distant. He recalled how, as he got older, he thought of himself as "a rational guy who had outgrown superstition."

When he needed help the most, though, his rational side fell short. "With middle age encroaching and the universe baring its teeth, I didn't know where to turn. I had fallen into a spiritual no man's land," he wrote.

His literary agent connected him with Newberg, who needed a collaborator for a book on the brain and religion. Passages in the book heightened his awareness, he said. "I can't say I've found religion," he conceded. "But I have come to realize that the biggest, most fascinating mysteries are to be savored, not resolved. And mystery is all around us: We just need to humble our hearts and pay attention."

Can't you see the problem? All the signs and indicators point to the existence of God, but that doesn't seem "scientific" to those *who want to find any other way* to interpret their own evidence!

Sadly, but tellingly, famous atheist writer Aldous Huxley spoke for too many scientists, intellectuals, popular personalities, and influential people in many scholarly fields when he said the following:

> I had motives for not wanting the world to have meaning; consequently I assumed that it had none, and was able without any difficulty to find satisfying reasons for this assumption.... For myself, as no doubt for most of my contemporaries, the philosophy of meaninglessness was essentially an instrument of liberation. The liberation we desired was simultaneous liberation from a certain political and economic system, and liberation from a certain system of morality. We objected to the morality because it interfered with our sexual freedom.

What About the Bible?

Now, dear reader, you may already be convinced that the Bible is the inspired Word of God, and absolutely accurate in all it says. You may not need further evidence. But then, you may have been derailed by latter-day skeptics who want to discredit it as scientifically, geologically, or even historically inaccurate, even suggesting or outright declaring that it's just a collection of fables or parables.

I've put in too much time, study, and personal investigation to let you keep doubting the obvious, logically rational truth that the Bible is what God Himself declares it to be: ***His inspired Word,*** by which ***we will be judged***!

So, here's another big **IF:**

IF you already believe what I've told you so far, you might be tempted to skip the next few pages. But please press on with me. I hope you're as deeply excited as I am that God knew we'd be surrounded by doubt and doubters, and has preserved all the truth any rational person could ever need to erase all of our doubts.

Scientific Truths Presented Long before Their Time

We mentioned earlier in the book the fact that scientific truths are revealed in the natural world, which repeatedly supports biblical people, places, beliefs, and events. We briefly looked at the example of Noah's ark, which science now reveals is sitting atop Mount Ararat in Turkey right now.

That's just one of many reports we can look at. For example, in many cases, writers such as David and Solomon and others mention physical, astronomical, and archaeological truths that were in direct conflict with the prevailing scholarly understandings of their times.

The earth's "shape." Consider, for example, Isaiah 40:22, which was written in approximately 700 BC: "It is God that sitteth upon the *circle of the earth.*"

Did you catch that? This passage indicates that the earth

is round, like a ball, in spite of the fact that, until roughly five hundred years ago, scientists believed the earth was as flat as an entrée at IHOP or a giant Frisbee!

If anyone thinks Isaiah was talking about a flat circle because he didn't more clearly reference a spherical object, consider this: Though others at the time believed the earth was flat, nowhere does Isaiah—or any other biblical writer, in the Old Testament or the New—use the word "flat" to describe the earth's shape. In Isaiah's time, there was no directly correlating word for "sphere." The closest choices in Hebrew were "circle" and "ball." The writers of the Bible were strong communicators. Then, as now, the concept of a "ball" connoted a small object that could be easily handled or manipulated. Elsewhere, Isaiah uses "ball" in exactly that context (see Isaiah 22:18, KJV). In Isaiah's time, one didn't think of a ball as stretching thousands of miles around. "Circle" was the more appropriate choice.

To answer skeptics on another front: The circle can't refer to the horizon, from Isaiah's point of view. Why? Let's check the entire verse: "It is God who sits above the circle of the earth. The people below must seem to him like grasshoppers. He's the one who stretches out the heavens like a curtain and makes his tent from them" (Living Bible). Clearly, this doesn't describe a bottom-up view from the prophet's perspective. The references to "people below" who "seem like grasshoppers" obviously connote a top-down "God view."

Though the ancient Greeks Pythagoras, Aristotle, and

Ptolemy speculated that the earth was round and put forth certain cosmological concepts (some accurate, some not), a comparison between their birth and death years and that of the Bible writers indicates that *all of the biblical writers predated* those Greek scholars by hundreds of years.[16]

The earth's "foundations." Over the centuries, many of the ancients believed earth had a foundation beneath it. For instance, some believed the earth was suspended on the heads of elephants. Others believed the mythical hero Atlas supported earth on his shoulders. Virtually no one believed earth was suspended in space.

Yet Job, some five thousand years ago, said, "God hangeth the earth upon nothing" (Job 26:7), clearly indicating otherwise. How could there be a "foundation" beneath earth if it "hangs" upon "nothing"? Skeptics have claimed that because Job referred to "foundations" in other passages of the book, he therefore believed earth itself had a foundation. The only problem with that is, in those passages, he used "foundation" in other contexts. As scholars have stated, Job is both a factual account of events and, in certain passages, it is poetic, lyrical, metaphoric prose. Job's references to "foundation" are clearly metaphoric—his way to help others understand what seemed impossible.

The earth's role in the cosmos. In the sixteenth century, astronomer Copernicus turned science upside down when he proved that the earth was not the center of our solar system, *but that the earth revolved around the sun.* At first, many resisted the discovery because they felt it contradicted the Bible. But the Bible never claimed the sun revolved around earth. If anything, the descriptions of earth in Job, Isaiah, and elsewhere support the truth of a planet that is *not* fixed in place, but part of an expanding cosmos!

Who knew?

GOD.

The earth's orderly creation. The very Genesis account of Creation and the order that God used to bring into existence our physical world is biologically and scientifically "right"—yet it conflicts head-on with all the other religions' accounts of how we all came to be and how our natural world was created, and it knocks the far-fetched hypotheses of evolutionists and many archaeologists into a cocked hat.

The account is told from an earthly perspective, in a way that people thousands of years ago could understand. The first verse of Genesis—"In the beginning, God created the heaven and the earth"—is what we'd today call a thesis statement. The chronology of Creation follows. The order given in that first verse—the heavens first, the earth second—is not insignificant. It is, in fact, geologically correct. A good deal of the known universe preceded earth and its solar system. Note that the verse doesn't say, "the earth and the heaven(s)." It easily could have, but it doesn't.

Genesis then describes the void prior to human creation ("the earth was without form, and void; and darkness was upon the face of the deep"). Next in the chronology, God continues creation. Genesis describes the sudden appearance of light, followed by creation of the heavens. (The King James Version's first use of the word "waters" is variously translated by scholars as gases, vapors, or a gaseous mass.) Genesis then describes the creation process on earth (we'll follow it with science's chronology). According to Genesis, marshes and trees appear, and animate life begins in water. Birds appear, among other creatures, then whales. Note the order: birds first, whales later (we'll come back to that in a minute). The oceans become more abundant with life, as does the earth. The next creatures mentioned are land mammals. A specific example—cattle—is given. Several similar unnamed animals are mentioned. Finally, man is created.

This occurs during different "days," which many scholars say represent epochs of time. Written about three and a half millennia ago, Genesis starts by describing a void and ends with the creation of man.

The earth's scientific creation. What does science say about how the world came into being? The Big Bang occurred, emitting light, as brilliant physicist Brian Greene illustrates in *The Fabric of the Cosmos.* The eventual formation of galactic systems also emitted light through the expanding universe. Among trillions of solar systems, planet earth formed, roughly 4.6 billion years ago.

About 4.5 billion years ago (by Greene's reasoning), the crust of the earth formed. Life developed in lakes and oceans, and the first primitive plants appeared on land. Millions of years later, the land became dominated by a range of plant life. Yet more millions of years after that, during the Jurassic Period, the first bird (archaeopteryx) appeared. Then, during the Eocene Period, some fifty-five to thirty-four million years ago, came the first whales, as well as early forms of the horse, rhinoceros, camel, and other hoofed animals. During successive periods, life forms proliferated. And finally, man appeared.

Review the previous information. As you do, compare the biblical and scientific chronologies and their basic similarities. But first, friend, keep in mind that—whether it took millions of years, as we count them, or six "days"—**God wasn't in a hurry.** In fact, the Psalmist David actually revealed in Psalm 90:4, "For You (God), a *thousand years are as a passing day, as brief as a few night hours.*"

The inescapable bottom line is that "somebody" had to be doing it, it wasn't happening by itself with no instigation, no intelligent design, and on only one little planet in the whole universe.

Who could the "somebody" possibly have been?

ONE GUESS.

The earth's life forms. Referencing the earth, the sun, and the moon, Genesis 1:9–19 describes the creation of our corner of the universe. The Bible's first reference to animate life appears in Genesis 1:20: "And God said, Let the waters bring forth abundantly the moving creature that hath life." This clearly indicates that life began in lakes and oceans. A closer look gives more information. "And God said, Let the waters bring forth abundantly the moving creature that hath life, and fowl that may fly above the earth."

Birds are referenced in verse 20, whales in verse 21. This is interesting because *the order is consistent with science's chronology*. Science says land mammals such as horses eventually predominate—also in basic agreement with Genesis, which references land mammals such as cattle. Finally, according to both science and Genesis, man comes on the scene. The account in Genesis isn't meant as an encyclopedic listing of every life form; it's a broad overview.

If the Genesis account were both myth and morality play, isn't it more likely that it would start with the creation of humans, since they're the dominant creatures on the planet? Since the Bible says humans have dominion over the animals of the earth, wouldn't humans as the first creation reinforce that more effectively if Genesis was a myth?

"When Moses wrote Genesis, Jews were just as ignorant of science as Hindus, the Chinese, or the Egyptians; yet here we find a record of creation" similar to scientific accounts of the last 150 years, biblical scholar T. J. McCrossan said. Genesis has the creation cycle beginning with the void and ending with man. Along the way are elements such as the appearance of early sea life, birds, whales, large land-based mammals, and mankind, in general alignment with science's chronology.

Question: Did Greene and other evolutionists "sneak a look at the Bible" before expounding their theories? Greene states, "Interestingly, the order agrees with science."

Historical/Geographical Truths Substantiate the Bible

The story of Moses, of course, is one of the most familiar accounts in the Old Testament. Some "scholars" have claimed the story was "made up by Jewish scribes to suit their own theological purposes—written late in Israel's history, between the seventh and third centuries BC."

None of these "scholars" was Jewish…surprise!

But according to a Discovery Channel documentary produced by the BBC, evidence is emerging that sheds new light on the Bible's accuracy.

Part of the problem in uncovering evidence of the story is the huge expanse of the Sinai desert. Intermittent wars in the area have also delayed archaeologists' work. But since the peace accords between Egypt and Israel in the late 1970s, archaeologists have resumed excavations that have produced promising results, according to the BBC.

One such site in the Sinai is the mountain of Serabit el-Khadim. Near the top of the mountain is a network of ancient mines, where slaves were brought from throughout Egypt to dig for the precious stone turquoise. Some of the slaves were Semitic, and very likely were Hebrews. Graffiti found on the walls is in Semitic, the language from which Hebrew is derived.

What's so significant about Semitic graffiti? It is evidence that Hebrews were in the Sinai and beyond, during the reign of the ancient pharaohs. Until recently, some scholars had mocked the story of Moses because no such evidence of Hebrews had ever been found.

Further, the Old Testament story of Moses begins in the Nile delta, where nomadic Hebrews had settled and become very populous and successful after Joseph gave them the best land of Goshen. Eventually, Joseph died, and as Exodus 1:8 records, "There arose a new king over Egypt, who did not know Joseph," who feared the growing might of the Jews. They were people of a different faith—dismissed as heretics by Pharaoh's court. The best way to control them, Pharaoh cynically concluded, was to use them as slaves.

Skeptics have claimed there's no evidence of Hebrew slaves in the delta. "But in recording the story," the BBC documentary noted, "the Bible adds small but telling details peculiar to life in the delta, which a later scribe, making the story up in Jerusalem, couldn't have known."

Case in point—Exodus 1:14: "And [the Egyptians] made their lives bitter with hard labor in mortar and bricks."

Delta houses are still built in the traditional way—from bricks made with mud and water and then allowed to dry. According to the BBC, "It was a common building technique in the Egyptian delta—but not in Jerusalem. Unless a Jewish scribe had an eyewitness account to go by, he wouldn't have picked up on this detail."

Authenticity of the Bible Itself

The original documents of the Old and New Testaments were copied by scribes and oracles, sometimes simultaneously. Over time, the copies were copied, "until at last some of those copies came into being which have remained to our own day as the earliest extant biblical manuscripts," according to scholar F. F. Bruce. "It is, in a way, surprising that so much biblical literature survived the adventures and vicissitudes experienced by the people of God throughout the early centuries. Most of it was written on very perishable material. It was exceptional for any part of Scripture to be incised on stone tablets, as the Ten Commandments were. That we have so many biblical texts from the period before the Babylonian exile approaches a miracle."

History records that the prophets and other authors took great care to preserve their work. "Isaiah, finding that his early messages went unheeded by king and people alike, wrote them down, sealed them, and entrusted them to his disciples, so that when at last his warnings came true the scroll could be unsealed and it would be recognized that he had prophesied truly."

The amazing discoveries of the Dead Sea Scrolls in 1947

and beyond also attest to the amazing accuracy of the copyists over periods spanning hundreds, and sometimes thousands, of years. The scrolls contained "the oldest surviving copies of Hebrew Scripture, dating from the closing centuries BC," Bruce noted.

This is what he has to say about the overall accuracy of the Bible, as evidenced by carefully rendered copies:

> The books of the Old and New Testaments are unparalleled among the literature that has come down to us from classical antiquity. Both in the abundance of this attestation and in the relatively short interval separating the earliest manuscripts from the original date of composition, the Bible is incomparably better served.

Notes

1. The Isaiah passage quoted is taken from both the NLT and NKJV versions to make Hebrew passages understandable in English—true to original meanings.
2. Pat Boone and Cord Cooper, *Questions about God and the Answers That Could Change Your Life* (Los Angeles, CA: Boone Books, 2009).
3. John Myers, *Voices from the Edge of Eternity* (New Kensington, PA: Whitaker House, 1968, 2012).
4. *Questions.*
5. Ibid.
6. In the Passover Seder He'd just left, He had passed the cup of wine to His disciples, saying, "This cup is the new covenant in my blood, which is shed for you."
7. Paraphrase of Exodus 3:13–14.

8. Josephus, *Antiquities of the Jews.*
9. Lee Strobel, *The Case for Christ* (Grand Rapids, MI: Zondervan, 1998).
10. Paraphrased.
11. The name of the book of Leviticus means: "Matters Pertaining to the Levites, the priestly tribe of the Jews, the ones who God made responsible for binding all the statutes and regulations on the people—and making sure they obeyed them."
12. Carl Gallups, *The Rabbi Who Found Messiah* (Washington, DC: WND Books, 2013).
13. In Jerusalem today is the "Dome of the Book"—the whole book of Isaiah is displayed under glass; it's in the form of the actual parchments found in the Dead Sea Scrolls two thousand years after they were carefully inscribed by very religious Jews in hiding. I've seen it; you can, too—but you'll have to know Hebrew to read it yourself).
14. *Questions.*
15. Ibid.
16. Ibid.